AF011361

WALKING IN GOWER

30 WALKS EXPLORING THE NATIONAL LANDSCAPE IN SOUTH WALES

by Andy Davies

JUNIPER HOUSE, MURLEY MOSS,
OXENHOLME ROAD, KENDAL, CUMBRIA LA9 7RL
www.cicerone.co.uk

© Andy Davies 2025
Third edition 2025
ISBN: 978 1 78631 284 6
eISBN: 978 1 78765 240 8
Second edition 2015
First edition 2012

Printed in Czechia on responsibly sourced paper on behalf of Latitude Press Ltd

A catalogue record for this book is available from the British Library
All photographs are by the author unless otherwise stated
© Crown copyright and database rights 2025 OS AC0000810376

Cicerone's EU representative for GPSR compliance is Easy Access System Europe, Mustamäe tee 50, 10621 Tallinn, Estonia. Email gpsr.requests@easproject.com.

To my mother and father, and family and friends who have shared this area with me.

Updates to this Guide

While every effort is made by our authors to ensure the accuracy of guidebooks as they go to print, changes can occur during the lifetime of an edition. Any updates that we know of for this guide will be on the Cicerone website (www.cicerone.co.uk/1284/updates), so please check before planning your trip. We also advise that you check information about such things as transport, accommodation and shops locally. Even rights of way can be altered over time. We are always grateful for information about any discrepancies between a guidebook and the facts on the ground, sent by email to updates@cicerone.co.uk.

Register your book: To sign up to receive free updates, special offers and GPX files where available, create a Cicerone account and register your purchase via the 'My Account' tab at www.cicerone.co.uk.

Front cover: Heatherslade and Fox Hole coves at low tide near Southgate

CONTENTS

Route summary table 6

INTRODUCTION 11
Geology 13
History 17
Wildlife habitats 21
Transport to and around Gower 26
Staying in Gower 26
Using this guide 26
GPX tracks 27

THE ROUTES
Walk 1   The Mumbles, Langland and Caswell 28
Walk 2   Caswell, Pwlldu and Bishopston Valley 36
Walk 3   Bishopston Valley 41
Walk 4   Pwlldu Head and Bishopston Valley 46
Walk 5   Pobbles, Three Cliffs Bay and Pennard Pill and Castle 51
Walk 6   Three Cliffs Bay, Pennard Pill, Ilston Cwm and Bishopston Valley . . 56
Walk 7   Pennard Pill, Three Cliffs Bay and Parc le Breos 63
Walk 8   Cefn Bryn, Broad Pool and Parc le Breos 68
Walk 9   Three Cliffs Bay, Tor Bay, Oxwich, Nicholaston Woods and Cefn Bryn 73
Walk 10 Millwood, Cefn Bryn, Reynoldston and Berry Wood 78
Walk 11 Penrice Castle, Cefn Bryn, Three Cliffs Bay and Oxwich NNR 82
Walk 12 Oxwich National Nature Reserve 90
Walk 13 Oxwich Point 93
Walk 14 Oxwich and Millwood 97
Walk 15 South Gower Cliffs and Port Eynon 103
Walk 16 Thurba Head and South Gower Cliffs 107
Walk 17 Rhossili Down, South Gower Cliffs and Port Eynon 113
Walk 18 Rhossili Down and Bay, Fall Bay and Mewslade Bay 120
Walk 19 Rhossili, Fall Bay and Mewslade Bay with Worms Head option . . . 126
Walk 20 Rhossili Down, Llanmadoc Hill and Broughton Burrows 131
Walk 21 Gower Coast NNR, Rhossili Down and Hardings Down 137
Walk 22 Mewslade Bay, Fall Bay, Rhossili Down and Hardings Down 146
Walk 23 Llanmadoc Hill, Llangennith, Burry Holms and Broughton Bay . . . 152
Walk 24 Llanmadoc Hill, Broughton Bay and Whiteford NNR. 157
Walk 25 Whiteford National Nature Reserve. 162
Walk 26 Landimore Marsh, Cheriton, Burry Pill and Weobley Castle. 166

Walk 27 Landimore Marsh, Arthur's Stone, Llanrhidian and Weobley Castle 169
Walk 28 Cefn Bryn, Llanrhidian and Weobley Castle. 175
Walk 29 Llanrhidian and Weobley Castle 179
Walk 30 Llanrhidian, Cilifor Top, Parc le Breos and Cefn Bryn. 182

Appendix A   Local points of interest index 186
Appendix B   Useful websites 187

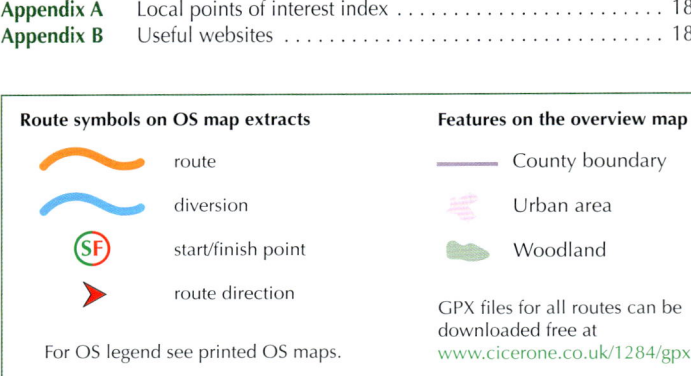

Acknowledgements

I would like to thank Stephen Parry and Chris Dale of the City and County of Swansea, for their help in clarifying Rights of Way. Owain Gabb of the Gower Ornithological Society kindly provided information on birds and Neil Barry, the Gower Society Footpaths Officer helped with some rights of way queries. Sean Hathaway of the City and County of Swansea kindly supplied information regarding Local Nature Reserves, and Jonathan Price, the Community Ranger for the Forestry Commission, provided valuable information and advice regarding Parkwood and Millwood. Thanks also go to Ben Evans for his help in preparing the section on geology. Thanks to my friend Ian Beaver for his company while researching the routes.

Finally, thanks to the team at Cicerone.

Sand dunes in Oxwich NNR looking east (Walks 9, 11 and 12)

ROUTE SUMMARY TABLE

Walk	Title	Start/Finish
1	The Mumbles, Langland and Caswell	Bracelet Bay (SS 6250 8715)
2	Caswell, Pwlldu and Bishopston Valley	Car Park, Bishopston (SS 5791 8926)
3	Bishopston Valley	St Teilo's Church, Bishopston (SS 5774 8937)
4	Pwlldu Head and Bishopston Valley	Southgate (SS 5540 8735)
5	Pobbles, Three Cliffs Bay, Pennard Pill and Castle	Southgate (SS 5540 8735)
6	Three Cliffs Bay, Pennard Pill, Ilston Cwm and Bishopston Valley	Southgate (SS 5540 8735)
7	Pennard Pill, Three Cliffs Bay and Parc le Breos	Parc le Breos (SS 5383 8963)
8	Cefn Bryn, Broad Pool and Parc le Breos	Penmaen (SS 5314 8877)
9	Three Cliffs Bay, Tor Bay, Oxwich, Nicholaston Woods and Cefn Bryn	Penmaen (SS 5314 8877)
10	Millwood, Cefn Bryn, Reynoldston and Berry Wood	Millwood car park (SS 4931 8825)
11	Penrice Castle, Cefn Bryn, Three Cliffs Bay and Oxwich NNR	Millwood car park (SS 4931 8825)
12	Oxwich National Nature Reserve	Car Park, Oxwich (SS 5029 8647)
13	Oxwich Point	Car Park, Oxwich (SS 5029 8647)
14	Oxwich and Millwood	Millwood car park (SS 4931 8825)
15	South Gower Cliffs and Port Eynon	Pilton Green (SS 4463 8713)
16	Thurba Head and South Gower Cliffs	Pilton Green (SS 4463 8713)
17	Rhossili Down, South Gower Cliffs and Port Eynon	Pitton Farm car park (SS 4268 8765)
18	Rhossili Down and Bay, Fall Bay and Mewslade Bay	Pitton Farm car park (SS 4268 8765)
19	Rhossili, Fall Bay and Mewslade Bay with Worms Head option	Rhossili Church car park (SS 4167 8807)
20	Rhossili Down, Llanmadoc Hill and Broughton Burrows	Rhossili Church car park (SS 4167 8807)

Route summary table

Distance	Total ascent	Time	Page
11.5km (7 miles)	220m	3hr	28
8.5km (5.4 miles)	110m	2hr 30min	36
6.5km (4 miles)	100m	2hr	41
6.5km (3.9 miles)	130m	2hr	46
6.5km (4 miles)	135m	2hr	51
17.5km (10.8 miles)	275m	5hr	56
6.5km (4 miles)	125m	2hr	63
13km (8.1 miles)	200m	3hr 30min	68
16.5km (10.2 miles)	290m	4hr 30min	73
10km (6.1 miles)	205m	2hr 30min	78
20km (12.4 miles)	410m	5hr 30min	82
4.5km (2.8 miles) to 10.5km (6.5 miles)	9m	1hr; 2hr 30min with extension	90
7.5km (4.6 miles)	155m	2hr	93
13km (8.2 miles)	230m	4hr	97
10.5km (6.5 miles)	140m	3hr	103
7km (4.5 miles)	45m	2hr	107
20.5km (12.7 miles)	325m	6hr	113
12km (7.4 miles)	250	3hr 30min	120
5.5km (3.3 miles) to 10km (6 miles)	60m	1hr 30min; 3hr with extension	126
16km (9.9 miles)	380m	4hr 30min	131

Walking on Gower

Walk	Title	Start/Finish
21	Gower Coast NNR, Rhossili Down and Hardings Down	Pilton Green (SS 4463 8713)
22	Mewslade Bay, Fall Bay, Rhossili Down and Hardings Down	Pitton Farm car park (SS 4268 8765)
23	Llanmadoc Hill, Llangennith, Burry Holms and Broughton Bay	Car park, Llanmadoc (SS 4398 9349)
24	Llanmadoc Hill, Broughton Bay and Whiteford NNR	Car park, Llanmadoc (SS 4398 9349)
25	Whiteford National Nature Reserve	Car park, Llanmadoc (SS 4398 9349)
26	Landimore Marsh, Cheriton, Burry Pill and Weobley Castle	Landimore (SS 4645 9353)
27	Landimore Marsh, Arthur's Stone, Llanrhidian and Weobley Castle	Landimore (SS 4645 9353)
28	Cefn Bryn, Llanrhidian and Weobley Castle	Cefn Bryn (SS 4907 9004)
29	Llanrhidian and Weobley Castle	Llanrhidian Church (SS 4976 9223)
30	Llanrhidian, Cilifor Top, Parc le Breos and Cefn Bryn	Llanrhidian Church (SS 4976 9223)

Route summary table

Distance	Total ascent	Time	Page
19.5km (12 miles)	380m	5hr 30min	137
14.5km (8.9 miles)	365m	4hr	146
13.5km (8.1 miles)	270m	3hr 30min	152
16km (10 miles)	235m	4hr 30min	157
10.5km (6.4 miles)	50m	2hr 30min	162
9km (5.5 miles)	80m	2hr	166
16km (10 miles)	160m	4hr 30min	169
10.5km (6.4 miles)	200m	3hr	175
5km (3.2 miles)	60m	1hr 30min	179
14km (8.7 miles)	310m	4hr	182

Going surfing in Rhossili Bay

Discarded dinghy at Bennett's Pill on the edge of Landimore Marsh (Walks 26 and 27)

INTRODUCTION

Rhossili Bay and Worms Head from Spaniard Rocks

Gower packs a glittering array of features into a remarkably compact and unspoilt area. Justifiably selected in 1956 as the UK's first Area of Outstanding Natural Beauty (AONB), this tiny South Wales peninsula boasts some of the most scenic beaches anywhere in the world, alongside fascinating geological formations, ancient archaeological sites and striking buildings from its more recent history.

An added bonus for holidaymakers wanting to stretch their legs, is the number of rich and varied walks that can be found in an area just 25km long by 13km wide, with spectacular landscapes easily accessible in all directions. The land abounds with interesting wildlife, geological and cultural features, and each walk described in this guidebook endeavours to capture this diversity and richness. A haven for walkers, photographers and nature lovers, Gower draws visitors back time and time again.

The peninsula is known for its spectacularly steep, rugged coastline and picture-perfect golden sandy beaches. But there is much more to Gower and the 30 circular routes described here will also take readers into the little-explored valleys, hills and ridges found inland. Many of the routes combine a section of coastal path, which may visit a secluded cove or wide-sweeping beach, with a ridge offering stunning panoramic views or with a tranquil stream valley. All avoid road-walking wherever possible.

Some coastal areas are well frequented, such as those around Langland, Oxwich and Port Eynon, but this guidebook focuses in the main on the lesser known parts where you will really be able to escape the crowds and find peace and solitude.

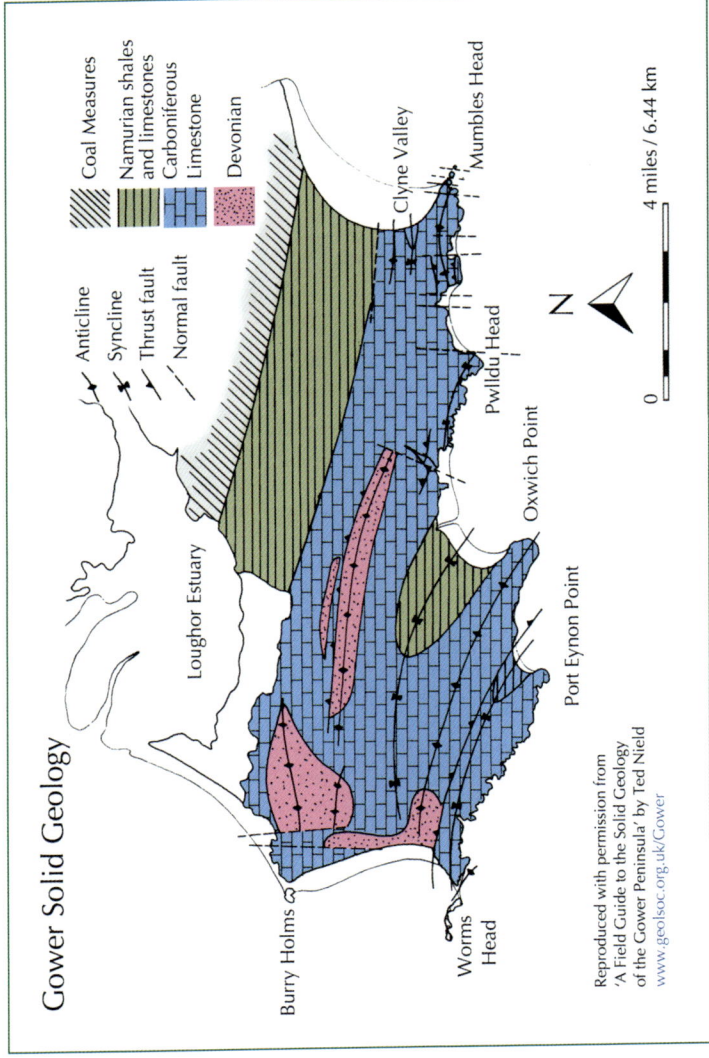

GEOLOGY

The continental plate on which Gower has formed was once situated south of the equator and has been drifting northwards over the past 425 million years. As a result, the sedimentary rocks that now comprise Gower were deposited under widely varying climatic conditions, from tropical seas rich in corals to coastal swamps.

The oldest rocks cropping out on Gower are from the end of the Devonian period and they form the cores of the major anticlines. During this period Gower lay in a region where sediment-laden rivers crossed a wide plain between mountains to the north and the sea to the south. The mountains were made of still older rocks whose roots now form much of central and north Wales. The climate at this time was tropical, possibly monsoonal, and the streams carried away coarse sediment from the intense erosion in the hills and deposited it across the braided river channels. In Gower we see pebbly rocks – conglomerates – at the top of the Devonian sequence overlying coarse sandstones, and these form the high ground of Cefn Bryn, Llanmadoc Hill and Rhossili Down.

The Devonian period ended approximately 360 million years ago

Middle and Outer Heads from the Inner Head (Walk 19 extension)

Bacon Hole bone cave and limestone rock strata (Walks 4 and 6)

when changing sea levels caused the sea to advance northwards. Initially mainly muddy marine sediments were laid down over the continental conglomerates, becoming dark, fine-grained shales, but gradually the amount of river-borne detritus diminished to leave clearer waters.

In these equatorial warm, clear waters, calcium carbonate precipitated in the form of shells and skeletons from the abundant corals, shellfish, brachiopods and crinoids (sea-lilies). This became the Carboniferous limestone series that comprises grey calcareous shales and massive limestones. The rocks are divisible into three groups: Lower Limestone Shales, Main Limestone and Upper Limestone Shales; however, there are many different rock types within these groups, each with varying textures, thicknesses and fossils as a result of subtle environmental changes. Overall it is about 800 metres thick, but becomes progressively thinner to the north, where the sea was shallower and more susceptible to interruptions of sedimentation as sea levels fluctuated, leading to the absence of some layers.

These stable conditions were interrupted around 320 million years ago by earth movements caused by approaching continents from the west and south. The compressive forces within the earth's crust caused the nearby landmass to be forced upwards and the increased rate of erosion flooded the limestone sea with sediments of sand, shale and mud from the river deltas.

Gower Stratigraphical Column

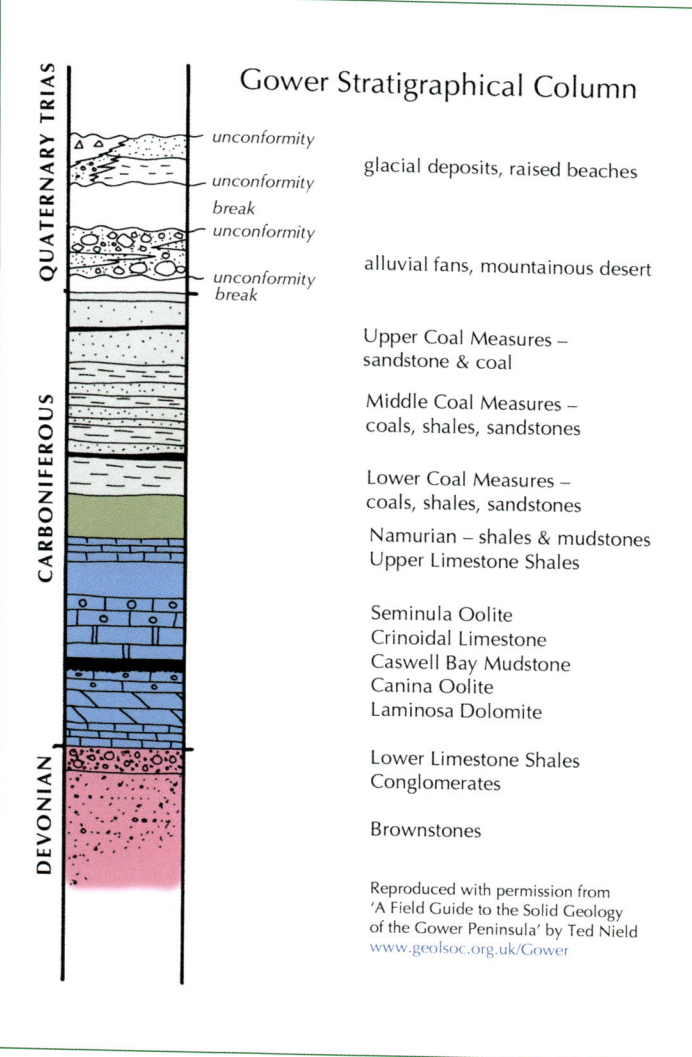

QUATERNARY / TRIAS
- unconformity
- glacial deposits, raised beaches
- unconformity
- break
- unconformity
- alluvial fans, mountainous desert
- unconformity
- break

CARBONIFEROUS
- Upper Coal Measures – sandstone & coal
- Middle Coal Measures – coals, shales, sandstones
- Lower Coal Measures – coals, shales, sandstones
- Namurian – shales & mudstones
- Upper Limestone Shales
- Seminula Oolite
- Crinoidal Limestone
- Caswell Bay Mudstone
- Canina Oolite
- Laminosa Dolomite

DEVONIAN
- Lower Limestone Shales
- Conglomerates
- Brownstones

Reproduced with permission from
'A Field Guide to the Solid Geology
of the Gower Peninsula' by Ted Nield
www.geolsoc.org.uk/Gower

View from the entrance to Bacon Hole bone cave (Walks 4 and 6)

This transition from limestone is marked by a coarse sandstone known as millstone grit, originally laid down by fast-flowing rivers. In its lower layers the gritstone contains massive white quartz conglomerates and sandstones, within which there are very pure bands of over 99 per cent quartz that were once worked for firebrick.

The next succession, the Coal Measures, originated in a widespread system of river deltas close to sea level, upon which grew lush tropical forests of giant mosses, horsetails and ferns that eventually became the coal. The Measures consist of sandstones, shales and coals arranged in a repeated sequence, as the forests flourished for a time, were inundated and buried by mud and sand as sea levels rose, and then developed once more on the river delta shales as the sea retreated.

These deposits are followed by massive beds of sandstone, known commonly to South Wales miners as the Farewell Rock, as they knew that there were no more workable coal bands once they had struck this distinctive geological marker.

The sedimentary layers of rock that form both Gower and the South Wales coalfield were folded to form a massive syncline some 280 million years ago, as a result of plate collisions further south that formed the super-continent Pangea. The older Devonian rocks have been exposed through erosion in the west and north of Gower, and Carboniferous limestone disappears beneath the Coal Measures to the north-east. There is also a series of tight folds that begins on the peninsula and continues under the Bristol Channel and into Devon.

The last major episodes to affect Gower were the Ice Ages, occurring during the last two million years of Earth history. During the Ipswichian interglacial period, around 130,000 to 120,000 years ago, the melting ice caused sea levels to rise to 6–9m above the present level. Subsequent falls in sea level left behind raised platforms, or raised beaches, containing beach deposits cemented with calcium carbonate. Where the beach deposit contains limpet shells among the rounded limestone fragments and sand it is known as the Patella raised beach. Many of the coastal caves open onto the platform of these beaches and it is likely that the caves were enlarged by wave action when they were at sea level.

Interior of Cathole Cave where cave art was discovered in 2010 (Walks 7 and 8)

HISTORY

The first humans to appear in Gower were small groups of nomadic hunters and gatherers who left behind little evidence of their visits as they moved through the landscape during the Palaeolithic era. Clues to their presence come from stone tools or waste from their manufacture. The chance find of a flint axe on Rhossili beach has pointed to human activity in this area as early as 125,000 years ago; then there is nothing until 100,000 years later, when further evidence for human presence is found, mainly from cave sites such as Cathole.

Excavations in the limestone caves have revealed evidence for Palaeolithic and Mesolithic activity, with the most famous of these being the 'Red Lady of Paviland'. This was in

Entrance to Goat's Hole, the burial site of the "Red Lady of Paviland" (Walks 16,17 and 21)

fact the burial of a Cro-Magnon man, the earliest known modern human, just before the final advance of the ice sheets 28,000 years ago in the Upper Palaeolithic. For around 15,000 years afterwards the climate was too cold for human occupation but, as the temperature warmed from around 13,000 years ago, people returned and the cave sites were again occupied by hunter-gatherer groups pursuing prey. There were probably no more than 50 people in the whole of Wales at this time, consisting of one or two extended families.

As the ice finally retreated around 10,000 years ago plant communities dominated by grass and sedge spread northwards. Many of the present-day plants found in the heathland and limestone grassland grew within these open communities, but by about 8500 years ago, when the climate was slightly warmer and drier than it is today, trees and shrubs, such as birch and pine followed by ash, oak, elm and hazel, had largely replaced them.

Mesolithic people are known to have fished and gathered shellfish when the coastline was only a few kilometres beyond its present location, with sea level rising rapidly to reach just 15–20m below its present-day height.

Evidence of activity is more plentiful during the Neolithic and Bronze Age periods as people began to construct various funerary monuments for their dead, such as chambered tombs and cairns like those in Parc le Breos and Sweyne's Howes. The communal graves and flint scatters suggest that groups of people inhabited the area during the Neolithic period. Pollen analysis from sediment cores shows signs of early forest clearance, a sign of Neolithic agriculture involving cultivating crops and possibly managing livestock.

Many enclosures were constructed on hilltops and coastal promontories during the Iron Age and the remains of earthwork banks and ditches are still visible. Limited excavation at a number of these sites has found evidence for domestic activity.

HISTORY

Iron Age pottery has also been recovered during the excavation of caves on Gower.

The Romans conquered the Silures, the dominant Iron Age Welsh tribe, in AD50 but there is surprisingly little structural evidence of Roman activity in Gower, even though there were military forts at Loughor to the north-east and Neath to the east. However, the recovery of Roman finds from the region, including two large coin hoards, illustrates that there was a degree of Roman activity on the peninsula; remains excavated near Oystermouth Church show the presence of a Roman Villa at this site. The Romans departed around AD410 allowing South Wales to revert to the Iron Age-like structure of small independent kingdoms.

Evidence of early medieval activity in Gower is attested to by a number of carved stones, such as those at Llangennith, Llanmadoc and Bishopston. These stones originate from early Christian sites with the Christian tombstone at Llanmadoc Church dating from around AD500. St Cenydd founded a small monastery at Llangennith in the 6th century but it was destroyed by Viking invaders and no structural evidence of it has been found. The Leper Stone in the porch of Llanrhidian Church has simple carvings of human figures and stylised animals and is thought to date from the 9th or 10th century.

Foxhole Slade Cave, Southgate (Walks 4, 5 and 6)

Aerial view of Iron Age fort above Bishopston Valley (Walks 2,3,4 and 6)

As a consequence of the Norman invasion many English settlers migrated across the Bristol Channel from the West Country into south Wales. Around 1106, the Norman King Henry I granted to Henry Beaumont, Earl of Warwick, the right to conquer the Welsh commote of Gwyr, which then extended between the rivers Tawe and Llwchr and as far north as the rivers Amman and Twrch. The Earl ruled Gwyr as a Marcher lordship, based at Swansea Castle, the control of which subsequently passed between a number of Norman families throughout the medieval period.

The Welsh fought back at least six times between 1113 and 1217 by burning the turf and timber castles, but they failed to take control of the peninsula. The strong stone castles still standing today at Oxwich, Penrice and Pennard were built at the end of the 13th century, and many village churches also date from this period. The castles were subsequently attacked and damaged by Owain Glyn Dwr's revolt between 1400 and 1413. Other evidence from the medieval period comes from the remains of strip field systems that can still be identified in parts of South Gower, the best example being the Viel at Rhossili.

Many farmhouses and associated out-buildings survive from post-medieval times. The large number of lime-burning kilns in the region reflects the agricultural activity during this period together with the associated remains of quarries, bell pits and collieries.

WILDLIFE HABITATS

Gower is extraordinarily rich in high-quality wildlife sites, boasting three National Nature Reserves, 24 Sites of Special Scientific Interest, 18 Wildlife Trust Reserves and three Local Nature Reserves. This is due to its diverse habitats that include large areas of salt-marsh and mudflat, woodland, stream valleys, moorland, sand dunes, cliffs, extensive intertidal rocky reefs and exposed and sheltered beaches.

The limestone cliffs, up to 70m high, of the south Gower coast are a classic botanical habitat, supporting large numbers of plant species that are nationally rare. A combination of geological, climatic and historical factors has contributed to this diversity. The limestone bedrock is a controlling factor in the creation of nutrient-poor thin soils and a varied geomorphology from vertical rock faces to incised clefts creates a variety of specialist niches. These habitats are influenced by the mild winters and cool summers, giving rise to a prolonged growing season.

Historic and present-day land use has left a surviving belt of semi-natural vegetation along the cliffs, unlike much of the UK where coastal areas have been ploughed right up to the cliff edge. Many species found here are unique to limestone grasslands as they are able to grow in the lime-rich thin soils. In turn, these plants attract a variety of insects which feed and lay eggs on them. Plants such as hoary rock-rose, spring cinquefoil, bloody cranesbill, viper's bugloss and greater knapweed along with insects like the silky wave moth occur here.

Pennard Pill with Pennard Castle (Walks 7, 9 and 11)

The south Gower cliff slopes are covered with numerous cracks and fissures created where rainwater has dissolved the limestone. Thin soils build up in the cracks, supporting specialised plants that are tolerant of the constant salty spray, such as sea plantain, thrift, rock samphire and sea beet. The cliffs all along south Gower contain some of the best examples of this habitat anywhere in the UK.

Tree mallow is found on the cliffs between Mewslade and Fall Bay, and the cliffs between Thurba and Deborah's Hole are a stronghold for yellow whitlowgrass, an alpine flower that blooms as early as the first week in March. It can also be found in narrow crevices in the upper cliffs between Pwlldu Head and Rhossili and on walls and rocks around Pennard Castle, but it occurs nowhere else in the UK.

Salt-tolerant plants grow on the lower part of the cliffs and include spring squill, golden samphire, rock sea-lavender, buck's horn plantain, sea campion, scurvygrass and the only maritime fern, sea spleenwort. Juniper, one of the most striking of the late-glacial relict species on Gower, can be found in places protected from cliff-top fires as it cannot regenerate, unlike gorse which then tends to replace it.

Maritime heath is found on the headlands and is a typical feature of the exposed Atlantic coast of Wales. Heather and western gorse grow together to form a dense habitat that turns purple and yellow with summer flowers. Patches of bare rock, grassland and bracken combine to make

Three Cliffs Bay at low tide and the cliffs of Great Tor in the distance (Walks 5 and 6)

WILDLIFE HABITATS

Clockwise from top left: Thrift or sea pink is a common sight on the coast in spring and summer; Common rock-rose grows on south Gower cliffs; the very rare yellow whitlow-grass flowering on the walls of Pennard Castle; Bloody cranesbill in flower in October on Worms Head; the salt-loving rock samphire; Yellow rattle growing in the meadow at Pilton Green car park; the red berries of the spindle tree

Devil's Bridge on Worms Head (Walk 19)

this a diverse habitat and a suitable home for many species of insects and scrub-nesting birds such as linnet, whitethroat, stonechat and yellowhammer. Stonechats are resident all year round and are frequent companions, darting from perch to perch from where they give their distinctive call. Other notable species include skylark, raven, chough, kestrel and peregrine falcon. Around 150 guillemots and small numbers of razorbill breed on Worms Head together with fulmar, shag and cormorant. Kittiwakes have decreased on the Worm but have populated Mumbles Pier.

Chough were absent for many years but returned to breed here in 1991 and are now a common sight, often announcing their presence by their call before they are in view. They like to feed on the closely cropped cliff-top turf, as do green woodpeckers. In 2001 a pair of Dartford warblers were discovered breeding near Port Eynon Point and they can now be found on the coastal cliff slope along south Gower. It is unusual among British warblers in that it is resident all year round; it is particularly fond of young gorse bushes as these contain an abundance of insects on which they feed.

The Loughor Estuary and Burry Inlet have the fourth largest salt marsh in Britain bounded by a number of limestone bluffs which were next to the sea 5000 years ago. The marsh developed in the shelter of Whiteford Burrows from east to west. The only

WILDLIFE HABITATS

Signpost in Bishopston Valley (Walks 2, 3, 4 and 6)

major area of salt marsh to be enclosed is Cwm Ivy Marsh when an earthen sea wall was built in 1638 which was later given a drystone facing.

The greatest number of plant species can be found along the upper fringes where the marsh merges with sand dunes, water meadows and freshwater marsh. Areas that are covered daily by the tides have a relatively small number of salt-tolerant species with areas nearest to low water dominated by glasswort, annual sea-blite and common cord-grass. The mid-marsh community comprises a closely grazed sward of common saltmarsh-grass with sea-purslane growing along the creek sides. This grades into the upper zone where the common saltmarsh-grass is mixed with red fescue, thrift and sea milkwort.

The highest part has a belt of tall sea rush which is some several hundred metres wide at Llanrhidian which has been traditionally cut by the farmers for bedding for their animals. Two plants worth searching out at the highest part of the grazed saltmarsh are the striking marsh mallow which has attractive pale pink flowers in July, and sea wormwood. Cwm Ivy Marsh is of particular interest as a lowland fen meadow and has tall stands of yellow flag iris.

The whole southern shore of the Burry Inlet is an extremely important wintering area for shorebirds, geese and duck. The area is best in winter with regular birds including black-tailed and bar-tailed godwits, snipe, jack snipe, lapwing, golden, grey and ringed plover, dunlin, knot,

View east of Nicholaston Burrows (Walks 9, 11 and 12)

sanderling, redshank, spotted redshank, curlew and oystercatchers. Ducks such as eider, wigeon, teal, pintail and long-tailed duck can be seen as well as red-breasted merganser, common and velvet Scoter, red-throated and great northern divers, shelduck, Brent geese and Slavonian and black-necked grebes.

Passerines are relatively few and far between, although there are plenty of meadow pipits and thrushes in winter, and a good range of woodland birds near Cwm Ivy. Raptors include hen harrier, peregrine, merlin, kestrel, buzzard and short-eared owl.

TRANSPORT TO AND AROUND GOWER

Gower is well served by the M4 motorway from the east and the west. There is a direct Intercity 125 train from Cardiff, Bristol and London, and regular buses from Swansea to the main villages. Contact Traveline Cymru on 0800 4640000 for more information or visit their website www.traveline.cymru/.

There are two main roads that run east–west along the peninsula, with a number of minor routes linking them north–south. Both the north and south Gower roads become severely congested during peak times in the summer school holidays.

STAYING IN GOWER

Gower is a mature tourist destination and is well served with all types of accommodation including hotels, bed and breakfast, self-catering, caravan parks and campsites. These often book up early, especially the best located campsites such as the one overlooking Three Cliffs Bay.

For up-to-date information contact Swansea Bay (www.visitswansea-bay.com).

USING THIS GUIDE

The walks in the book are arranged in a clockwise order around the peninsula, starting in the south-east at Mumbles and finishing in the north-east at Llanrhidian. It is designed to be used in conjunction with the OS Explorer® 1:25,000 Gower Sheet 164. The 30 routes described are of varying lengths and degrees of difficulty to cater for different interests and abilities and a fit walker will not find any of the routes particularly strenuous. All the routes are circular, only use roads where unavoidable, and explore little frequented areas wherever possible.

Rights of way are generally well-marked and, on the whole, provide a good and even walking surface. Routes that include non-coastal sections can vary considerably in their nature depending on the amount of rain that has fallen. Good quality waterproof boots are recommended under these circumstances, but stout walking shoes will suffice during the drier summer months.

Gower is exposed to prevailing south-westerly winds and the weather can change rapidly at any time of the year but temperatures are moderated by the relatively warm sea water of the Atlantic Drift. As a consequence, winters are seldom severe although the summits can provide a surprisingly mountain moorland experience on a hard snowy day. It is wise to carry enough clothing in case the weather changes. Multiple thin layers will give you more flexibility to respond to changing conditions.

Routes are illustrated with extracts from the 1:50,000 OS® maps, with the main route marked in orange and any alternative or extension routes marked in blue. Alternative and extended routes are described within the main route description. Features along the walk that appear on the map are highlighted in bold in the route description. The route descriptions are also accompanied by information boxes which are cross-referenced to other route descriptions, using the walk number.

GPX TRACKS

GPX tracks for the routes in this guidebook are available to download free at www.cicerone.co.uk/1284/GPX. If you have not bought the book through the Cicerone website, or have bought the book without opening an account, please register your purchase in your Cicerone library to access GPX and update information.

A GPS device is an excellent aid to navigation, but you should also carry a map and compass and know how to use them. GPX files are provided in good faith, but in view of the profusion of formats and devices, neither the author nor the publisher accepts responsibility for their use. We provide files in a single standard GPX format that works on most devices and systems, but you may need to convert files to your preferred format using a GPX converter such as gpsvisualizer.com or one of the many other apps and online converters available.

WALK 1
The Mumbles, Langland and Caswell

Start/finish	Bracelet Bay (SS 6250 8715)
Distance	11.5km (7 miles)
Total ascent	220m
Time	3hr
Refreshments	Forte's Ice Cream Parlour, Plunch Lane; cafés in Rotherslade and Langland; shops and pubs in The Mumbles.

The walk follows the cliff path west from Bracelet Bay to Langland and Caswell before heading inland through Bishop's Wood, returning to the start via Oystermouth Castle and Mumbles Head. The footpath to Caswell is along a tarmac surface with the route becoming a little boggy crossing a short section of Clyne Common. There are plenty of opportunities for refreshments along the way and two beautiful beaches for a swim.

Bracelet Bay and Mumbles Lighthouse

WALK 1 – THE MUMBLES, LANGLAND AND CASWELL

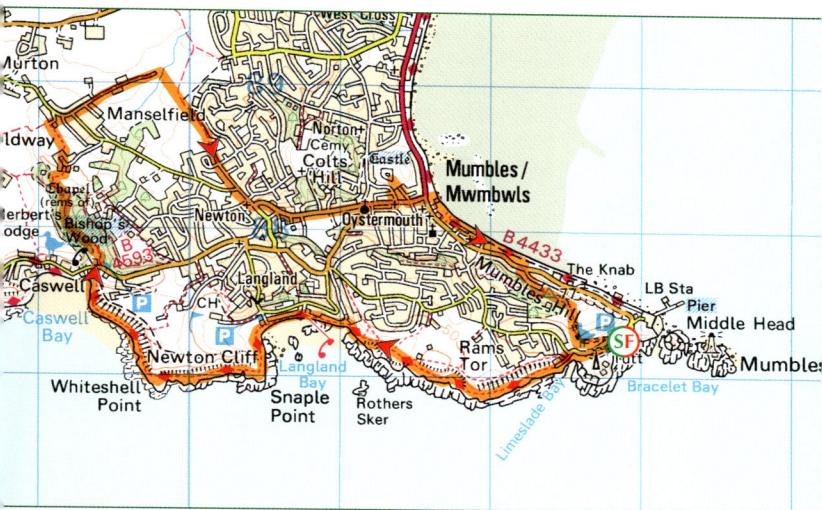

With Bracelet Bay on your left, take the road to the west and bear left at the turning to Plunch Lane and pass in front of Forte's Ice Cream Parlour on your right. The road soon ends and becomes the cliff path. In the rocky cove of **Limeslade** there is a sandy beach at low tide with interesting rock pools. The rocks here are made of Carboniferous limestone.

Just up Plunch Lane is a house built by Catherine Zeta-Jones and Michael Douglas. On the headland to the east is the aerial and building of the Mumbles Coastguard station. Beyond is Bracelet Bay and **Mumbles Head**. The lighthouse was built on the Outer Head, the last island of three, in 1794 and is accessible by foot at low tide. The light was originally lit by two open coal fires arranged vertically to distinguish it from other beacons. These were replaced by an oil lantern and lens creating two beams.

Mumbles Head Fort was constructed next to the lighthouse in 1860 in anticipation of an invasion by Napoleon III of France which never came to fruition. It was used again during World War 2 by a small battery of soldiers. Bob's Cave can be found at the tip of Mumbles Head. Normally only noticeable from the sea, it is possible to reach the cave during low tide. **Exercise extreme caution with the incoming tide.** Remains of bison and buffalo from the Neolithic period and signs of human habitation were discovered during excavations in the cave, which was named after a member of the Mumbles Lifeboat crew, Bob Jenkins, who was found sheltering there two days after a tragic rescue attempt in January 1883.

Looking back east along this path you can see that the rocks, arranged in parallel layers or beds, have been tilted by around 45 degrees to the south. Inland there is a **Local Nature Reserve** covered mainly in gorse.

The path climbs steeply up to **Rams Tor**, giving great views of the coastline to the west of Caswell Bay, Pwlldu Bay and, finally, Oxwich Point. From Rotherslade, where there is a café, you can either continue along the path to Langland or walk across the beach if the tide is low enough.

Langland Bay is a designated conservation area with 75 Edwardian beach chalets overlooking the sandy beach. Notice an impressive building with a green turret behind the beach. This is a Scottish Baronial-style mansion built in the mid-19th century by the Crawshay family, the Merthyr Tydfil Ironmasters, as their summer residence.

Continue along the coastal path towards Caswell Bay. To the right are **Newton Cliffs** and Summerland Cliffs Local Nature Reserve. Rare plants such as hoary rockrose exist within this calcareous grassland, itself a rare habitat within the UK.

Chalets at Langland built in the 1920s by the Council

Caswell Bay at low tide

The path climbs up to Whiteshell Point from where there is a fine view west of Caswell Bay, Brandy Cove and Pwlldu Bay. Notice the furrows running down the cliffs between the bay and Pwlldu Head. These were once quarried for limestone (see Walk 2). Brandy Cove was famous for smuggling.

Cross over the road into the car park and follow the path that runs along the valley on its left-hand side into **Bishop's Wood** to a wooden building with a turf roof. The path on the right tends to be muddy in winter.

From the roundhouse, take the path on the left that soon joins another. Ignore the path that comes down from the right. Cross over this bridleway and take the lower path. Ignore the first turning on the right and take the second, by a sign for Lanwell, which then crosses a boardwalk. Just before you turn off, you may want to explore the area marked St Peter's Well on the 1:25,000 map where there are remains of a **chapel**. There is a turf-covered roundhouse on the left and the land here is used for running courses in traditional woodland management.

Once over the boardwalk, ignore the path on the left and continue up the slope. This area has a number of interesting wooden houses.

Cross diagonally over the green and follow the footpath that then swings left and runs between two hedges. Ignore the path that crosses the open field.

When you reach a track turn right into **Manselfield**. When the road bends round to the right carry straight on along Reigit Lane. Ignore the turning on the right to Mansel Drive and carry on past the end of the houses and onto a footpath

OYSTERMOUTH CASTLE

Oystermouth Castle in Mumbles

The Castle was founded by William de Londres of Ogmore Castle early in the 12th century and this was probably a ringwork and bailey on the highest part of the hill. The earliest stone building of the castle, the keep, dates from the 12th century. The Welsh burnt this early castle twice, in 1116 and 1215.

In the 13th century the de Braoses were lords of Gower and held the castle, and towards the end of the century Oystermouth rather than Swansea became their principal residence. Rhys ap Maredudd attacked and burnt Swansea and captured Oystermouth in 1287. Extensive repairs and extensions to the castle were made for the visit of Edward I on 10 and 11 December 1284. The de Braoses rebuilt the castle in stone, and most of what remains today is from that period.

---

that comes to a gate to Clyne Common. Continue straight ahead along the path, cross a boggy area and turn right in the direction of the red houses ahead and then in the direction of two mobile phone masts. The path becomes indistinct in places and finally crosses a boggy area to a swing gate. Follow the path to the road and carry straight on.

> Look out on your right for **Paraclete Congregational Church**. Dylan Thomas's uncle was the preacher here, and as a child Dylan was forced to attend Morning Service, Sunday School and sometimes Evening Service. He drew on these experiences in his poetry and his uncle's fire and brimstone style of preaching influenced Thomas's declamatory style of delivery on the radio and in public performances. Needless to say, Thomas also frequented the Newton Inn.

WALK 1 – THE MUMBLES, LANGLAND AND CASWELL

Turn left with the Newton Inn on the corner with the Rock and Fountain on your right and drop down the hill to Mumbles. Turn left just after passing Mumbles Baptist Church on your right to visit **Oystermouth Castle**.

The bench in front of the castle is a great vantage point from which to take in all the features of the village. The **Mumbles** is thought to have been named by the Romans after the two islands that complete the sweep of the bay, their resemblance to breasts giving rise to *mamma* in Latin and *mammelles* in French. Archaeological finds show that the area was being cultivated over 3000 years ago. Two well-finished axe-heads have been found at Newton and Mumbles Hill and the remains of a mosaic floor of a Roman villa were uncovered in 1860 during excavations for an extension to All Saints Church.

As far back as the late 17th century Swansea Bay was reputed to have the best bed of **oysters** in Great Britain with the first records of oysters dating back to Roman times. The heyday of the trade was from 1850 to 1873, with the oysters being sold in Bristol, Gloucester, Liverpool and London. At its peak in 1871, nearly 16 million oysters were landed; the industry supported around 600 people with 500 of these manning the 180 skiffs. Unfortunately, it attracted many outsiders and larger boats from London and France plundered the beds leading to a drastic decline in the industry from the mid-1870s.

The other main industry was **limestone quarrying** in the 16th and 17th centuries. The stone was burnt using coal to produce lime, an agricultural fertiliser for acid soils. Lime was transported by boat to Neath, Baglan and across the Bristol Channel to Somerset and Devon.

From the castle drop down the grassy slope to the road and continue straight on to join the road through the village. Turn left and descend between the shops and cross over the Mumbles Road in front of the White Rose. Turn right and walk along the seafront, probably in the footsteps of Dylan Thomas. This was the route of the old Mumbles Train which ran along the promenade to the terminus at Mumbles Pier.

Dylan Thomas, Swansea's famous poet, was a frequent visitor to Oystermouth and describes his evenings there in his early biographical letters. He was supposed to be rehearsing with the local amateur dramatic group, the Swansea Little Theatre, with short breaks for refreshment in one of the many pubs along the seafront. In reality, he spent much of his time drinking 'oystered beer' in the Antelope, The Marine (now the Village Inn) and the Mermaid which was destroyed in a fire.

THE MUMBLES TRAIN

The Oystermouth Railway was built in 1804 to move limestone from the quarries of Mumbles, iron ore from a mine near Knab Rock and coal from the Clyne Valley to Swansea and to the markets beyond. It carried the world's first fare-paying railway passengers in 1807 and later became the Swansea and Mumbles Railway.

Horse-drawn railway carriage on the Mumbles Railway c.1865. Reproduced by permission of Blackpill Local History Society

The first carriages were hauled on tracks by horses but a turnpike road was established alongside the railway in the mid 1820s that deprived it of much of its business, and the passenger service ceased in 1827. The track was relaid with conventional rails in 1855 and the horse-drawn passenger service was reinstated between Swansea and the Dunns, Oystermouth.

Steam-powered locomotives were introduced in 1877 and the line was extended to Southend in 1893 and to the pier in 1898. From 1900 to the 1920s the railway usually carried up to 1800 passengers each single journey, another world record at the time, but the enormous load meant a maximum speed of 5mph.

The pier was built in 1898 and, at 225m long, is a fine example of Victorian architecture. It was the western terminus for the Mumbles Train, linking it with the White Funnel paddle steamers that carried passengers on routes along the River Severn and the Bristol Channel.

The train line was electrified in 1929 and passengers were carried by a fleet of double-decked cars, each with a capacity of 106. An astonishing 5 million passengers were carried in 1945. Sadly, the last train ran in 1960, and despite many campaigns to resurrect it, it seems that it is lost for ever.

Leave the promenade just before the George Inn where there is a footpath sign 'Mumbles Hill Local Nature Reserve' indicating the route up some stone steps alongside a row of old cottages. This steep climb brings you to a path at the top where you turn left. Follow the top of the cliff with a great view of the sweep of Swansea Bay and Port Talbot.

The beauty of **Swansea Bay** has often been compared with that of the Bay of Naples and was described by Dylan Thomas, as 'a long and splendid curving shore'. Part of the Bristol Channel, it has one of the largest tidal ranges in the world at 10.5m.

This area is a Local Nature Reserve and habitat types include maritime heath, limestone grassland, limestone scrub and woodland, each supporting different plants and animals. Over 200 species of plants and fungi, 40 species of birds and hundreds of species of insects have been recorded on the Hill.

A Neolithic stone axe head was discovered in an allotment in 1938 and a fissure on the hill has also revealed prehistoric human bones and teeth. A military camp was established during the Second World War and remnants of the 623rd Anti-Aircraft Battery gun emplacements and control bunker are still visible.

Drop down the seaward side of the hill along the obvious track to the road above Bracelet Bay.

This bay is a geological Site of Special Scientific Interest and is worth exploring. The rocky outcrops provide excellent exposures of **geological structures** formed during the Variscan mountain-building episode up to around 280 million years ago. The exposures show a cross-section through the core of a major upward fold structure, the Langland Anticline, which extends across the whole Gower Peninsula, bringing the Carboniferous limestone to the surface. The study of this area has greatly increased our understanding of this period of geological activity in South Wales.

Turn west to return to the start.

WALK 2
Caswell, Pwlldu and Bishopston Valley

Start/finish	Car park, Bishopston (SS 5791 8926)
Distance	8.5km (5.4 miles)
Total ascent	110m
Time	2hr 30min
Refreshments	Joiners Arms and Valley Inns and Spar in Bishopston; The Plough and Harrow Inn and Village Stores in Murton; cafés in Caswell.

This route gains the coast via Bishop's Wood Nature Reserve at Caswell Bay and then runs along the base of the cliffs to Brandy Cove and Pwlldu Bay. Tales of smuggling and ghosts abound here and one can just imagine the locals dodging the excise men by bringing their illicit booty ashore under the cover of darkness. Pwlldu Bay is also steeped in industrial history, as is Bishopston Valley which once had a working lead mine. The stream plays cat-and-mouse by disappearing and reappearing again a number of times.

From the car park in **Bishopston** walk up the road, past the Valley Inn and Joiners Arms on Bishopston Road.

The house called Marston, no. 133, was **Dylan Thomas's father's home** when he moved from Cwmdonkin Drive following his retirement from teaching at Swansea Grammar School in 1937. Dylan and his wife Caitlin were frequent guests and it was here, in 1941, that Dylan wrote the poem *The Ballad of the Long Legged Bait*.

Turn left just past the Spar down Providence Lane. Follow this and cross over a road in a housing estate to the Plough and Harrow pub. Bear left and then right around the pub to Murton Green. Turn right just past the Wesleyan Methodist Church and follow the road to a bend. Follow the footpath sign to Caswell Bay ignoring the turn to Clyne Common.

The track comes to a Y-junction where you bear left and keep left again a few metres on. Drop down the sunken track, and when it bends to the right, continue on the main track between the two hedges. On your left you can see a stone

WALK 2 – CASWELL, PWLLDU AND BISHOPSTON VALLEY

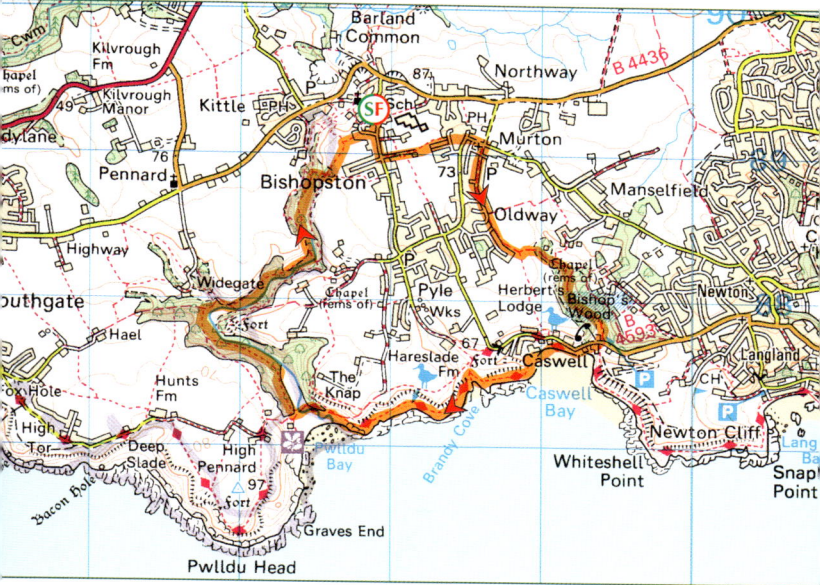

building which is the remains of a chapel at St Peter's Well. Further along this sunken lane you can see a turf-roofed roundhouse. This is Lanwell where courses in traditional woodland management are run.

Once you reach the valley floor turn right, pass the roundhouse and follow the path to **Caswell** through **Bishop's Wood** Local Nature Reserve. Cross over the road and see if the tide is low enough to walk around the rocks on the right. If not, walk right up the road and turn left onto the Coast Path next to the entrance to a majestic house.

Drop down to the beach and skirt along the base of the pebbles and climb up the steps in the corner. Turn left at the top and follow the path above the tops of the cliffs, taking care here as there is a steep drop adjacent to the route.

Coming around the point, if the tide is low, there is a superb view of the inclined rock layers in the intertidal limestone reef. On your right is **Redley Cliff**, a nature reserve owned by the Wildlife Trust for South and West Wales and is part of the Caswell Bay Site of Special Scientific Interest.

PWLLDU QUARRYING

The cliffs to the west of this beautiful bay have been extensively modified by quarrying up to the beginning of the 20th century. Rights of 'cliffage' were awarded to farming tenants who could quarry the limestone from the slopes of Pwlldu Head, which was then shipped across the Bristol Channel to Devon where it was burned to make agricultural lime.

The quarried stone was piled a short way from low water and marked with a post. Ships then sailed into the cove at high tide, located the posts and remained there until the tide dropped, leaving the ship beached and ready to be loaded before the next high tide. Some of the ships may have actually been scuttled by opening the sea cocks before the tide had fully dropped. As the ship beached the sea cocks would be closed with water partially filling the hold of the ship, breaking the fall of the cargo of rock as it was loaded. The remaining water would be drained out before the tide returned.

The houses nestling at the head of the beach were once four pubs serving the thirsty workers. The large white house was the Beaufort Arms and opposite it was the Ship Inn, but the Bull and New Inn are no longer in existence.

Continue along to the next inlet of **Brandy Cove** which gets its name from stories of smugglers using the bay to unload their illegal tobacco and alcohol during the 18th century. There is a raised beach exposed below the path and an area of scree on the western side above the path.

Old stone barn at Pwlldu Bay with former Beaufort Inn behind

WALK 2 – CASWELL, PWLLDU AND BISHOPSTON VALLEY

There are a couple of **legends of the supernatural** associated with the beach. One is about a witch called 'Old Moll' who lived in the caves near the beach and spent much of her time wandering through the many small villages and farms on Gower. The other story is connected to a chilling real-life murder that took place near the beach in 1919. Nearby villagers claimed that they could hear screams coming from the caves near the beach at night.

Coming around into **Pwlldu Bay** there is a good view of the tilted limestone rock strata along the foreshore at low tide and the old quarry in the cliff on the western side of the bay. Turn left where the path joins a track and cross the stream using the bridge. The bay is worth exploring by turning left here for its shingle beach and past history associated with quarrying and with smuggling (see Walk 3).

Continue by turning right once over the bridge, following the path past the National Trust sign along the western bank of the stream. Ignore the sign to Southgate where a valley joins from the left, once used to smuggle contraband to the Highway Farms in Southgate, and follow the sign to Bishopston and Kittle.

Continue following the path in the valley signposted Kittle Church, ignoring the two bridges. Look out for where the stream divides into three and disappears underground. Shortly after, ignore the sign for Kittle and continue along the valley floor, signposted Church Lane. Notice that the stream-bed is dry but it will hold water in extreme spate conditions.

The path crosses the stream-bed and passes over an old stone wall. Look out for some stone ruins well disguised with moss. Just beyond up to the right is an old mine adit.

The dry stream bed upstream of Guzzle Hole

WALKING ON GOWER

Autumn in Bishopston Valley

Listen out for the sound of falling water which is coming from **Guzzle Hole** over to your left. Again, in times of spate, water gushes out of this cave, and also comes in from the right if the massive sink hole further up the valley cannot cope with the extreme flood.

Continue along the dry stream-bed, ignoring the sign for Kittle on the left up the steps. Just after this, turn right and climb the steep slope out of the valley. Once you have climbed out of the valley, ignore the footpath on the right and continue following the wall to a stile. Follow the footpath across the field and, at the dwellings, take the track straight ahead which brings you to the Joiners Arms and The Valley pub in **Bishopston**.

Alternatively, it is worth carrying on a little way further up the stream-bed in the valley to see the sink hole and, if conditions have been dry, you can continue to follow the stream-bed to St Teilo's Church where you turn right and up to the Joiners Arms and The Valley pub in **Bishopston**.

Turn left back to the start.

WALK 3
Bishopston Valley

Start/finish	St Teilo's Church, Bishopston (SS 5774 8937)
Distance	6.5km (4 miles)
Total ascent	100m
Time	2hr
Refreshments	Joiners Arms and The Valley pub in Bishopston

This route explores the beautiful and interesting Bishopston Valley which culminates in the remote cove of Pwlldu Bay. Good food and beer can be enjoyed at the Joiners Arms and The Valley pub near the end of the walk, the former having its own micro-brewery. Another four pubs were thriving at Pwlldu when the quarry here was active. The route follows the valley where the stream disappears and reappears depending on water levels as it crosses the Carboniferous limestone.

Start at **St Teilo's Church** where there is plenty of space for car parking. Part of the route to the swallow hole is along the stream-bed; after periods of heavy rain the stream may be flowing and you will have to make a detour. If the stream-bed is dry or there is only a small flow, take the footpath on the opposite side and follow the path; this uses the stream-bed at first, after which there is a path on the other bank to the swallow hole.

Detour to avoid the stream
If the stream is flowing, cross the bridge by the side of the ford, climb Old Kittle Road and turn left opposite the Beaufort Arms onto the track by the side of the green. Pass between the houses and, leaving the National Trust sign on your left, follow the track to Great Kittle Farm. Take the path to the left of the entrance and follow this to where it divides and take the one that drops down the middle of the gully.

Pass a fenced-off area where you will find a large limestone cavern. Once you've reached the bottom of the Bishopston Valley, which is surprisingly dry with no stream, turn right, signposted Pwlldu. You have now rejoined the main route. If you wish to see the impressive swallow hole, turn left and walk for 250m.

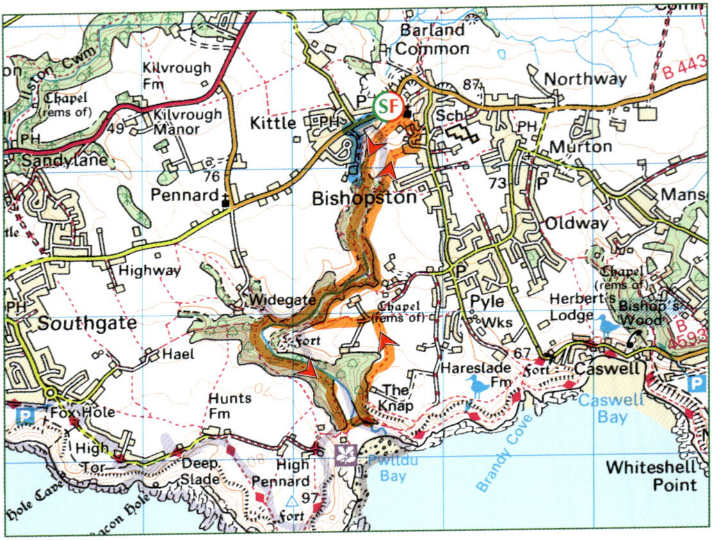

WALKING ON GOWER

Entering the National Trust-owned Bishopston Valley from Pwlldu

BISHOPSTON VALLEY

The gated entrance to Long Ash Mine

The underlying geology is Carboniferous limestone, resulting in classic karst features at the surface. The Bishopston Pill disappears and reappears a number of times along the length of the valley, creating caves with magical names such as Guzzle Hole.

The stream disappears underground near Barlands Quarry, leaving the stream-bed and ford below St. Teilo's Church dry except in periods of high rainfall. There is a rock exposure of the Namurian limestone here. Just south of this is a vast pit with sheer walls and a sink hole in its bottom. A little way along from this, the stream-bed is obviously only infrequently flooded and the valley itself is narrow and gorge-like.

On the opposite side of the valley from Guzzle Hole is Long Ash Mine, an adit around 60m in length, which was abandoned in 1854. This produced lead and silver from a lode formed by mineralisation along a fault. It was never extensively worked, probably due to its tendency to flood. A short distance further up the dry floor of the valley from the mine is the entrance to Guzzle Hole where you can see the stream running underground.

The **swallow hole** is an impressive feature. The stream leading to it is only active during or after heavy rain, and even then the water often disappears just before it reaches the cliff edge where it would form a waterfall. Under exceptional circumstances this enormous hole fills with water and the stream overflows down the valley.

Walking on Gower

PWLLDU BAY SMUGGLING

Smuggling was commonplace during the 18th and early 19th centuries; of the two secluded houses at Pwlldu, the Beaufort Inn is reputed to have had dealings with smugglers who used its cellar for free storage. The arrangement the landlord had was that fewer barrels left than entered.

One local historian claims that more contraband was landed here than anywhere else in the Bristol Channel. The sheltered bay offered an ideal location for these illegal activities, with the wooded Bishopston Valley providing plenty of cover for transporting contraband to the farms at Highway; these were used as staging posts and as headquarters for the smuggling company.

Walking down the steep-sided valley, the stream-bed is very uneven, and after periods of heavy rain you will see water gradually starting to flow in the bed. When this changes character to being smoother you will see another dry stream course on your right, at the head of which is a cave called Guzzle Hole where you will be able to hear and see the underground stream. About 60m further down the valley, the path rises a little and there is a gated entrance to a mine adit, the Long Ash Mine.

Continue down the valley, cross the dry stream-bed and just further along you will discover the resurgence where the water emerges from three underground passageways called sumps. Follow the path to Pwlldu Bay, ignoring two bridges

Guzzle Hole where Bishopston Pill can be seen flowing underground

Aerial view of the buildings at Pwlldu Bay

that cross the stream and a side valley on the right. When the route comes to a National Trust sign at **Pwlldu Bay** there is a bridge down to your left and a path climbing up the right. To explore the Bay, take the path that drops down to the bridge; do not cross, but head for the houses ahead. Pwlldu is full of interest for its shingle beach, smuggling and quarrying.

Cross the bridge and take the track up the side of the valley. Leave this by taking a footpath on the left through the wood to where it meets another path at Knapp Farm. Turn left and pass through a number of swing gates until you come to where the path enters a field with the rugby posts of South Gower RFC on your right. Keep to the hedge on your left to a road. Turn left here on to a bridleway, pass Backingstone Farm on your right and shortly afterwards bear right continuing on the bridleway.

Turn right when you meet the gate and take the footpath which follows the edge of the valley. Do not take the path that drops down the valley side. At the head of a gully there is a white house. Continue along the path following the valley edge. This brings you into a field where you keep to the left hedge and to a gully. Cross over a fence and a low stone wall and turn right, cross a stile and follow the footpath across the field. At the dwellings take the track straight ahead which brings you to the Joiners Arms and The Valley pub.

Take the path with Prospect Barn on your left down the slope to a road and a house, turn left and take the footpath to the left of the house. This skirts around the graveyard and drops down back to the start at St Teilo's Church.

WALK 4
Pwlldu Head and Bishopston Valley

Start/finish	National Trust car park, Southgate (SS 5540 8735)
Distance	6.5km (3.9 miles)
Total ascent	130m
Time	2hr
Refreshments	Three Cliffs Café and stores at the start
Note	Care must be taken near cliff edges, especially in poor visibility or if children and dogs are in tow

The route heads along East Cliff to High Tor, with fine views west of Oxwich Bay, and then on to Pwlldu Head from where there is a grand vista of Caswell, Mumbles Head and the Vale of Glamorgan coastline as far as Nash Point. This part of the walk is made more interesting by following pathways as close to the cliff line as possible as this affords the best views, and also crosses an Iron Age fort. After visiting the old quarry village at Pwlldu the route turns inland, following the picturesque Bishopston Valley with its enjoyable woodland walk.

Foxhole Slade Cave, Southgate

WALK 4 – PWLLDU HEAD AND BISHOPSTON VALLEY

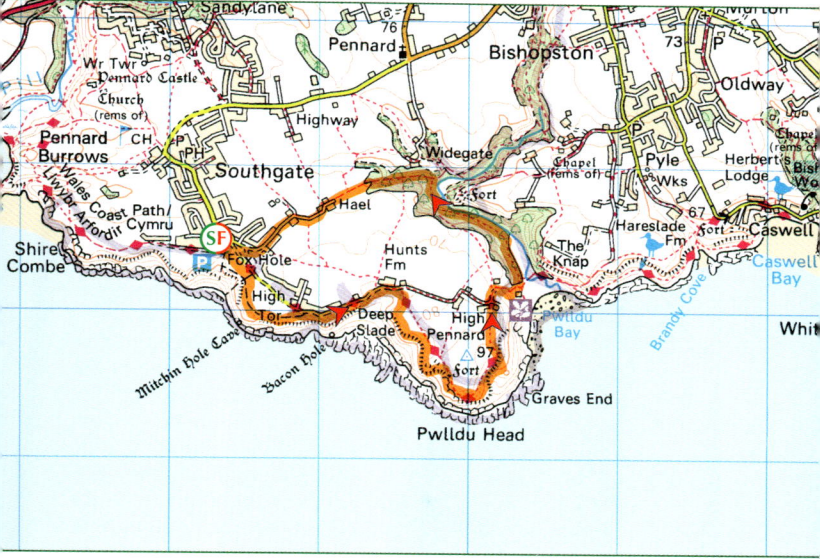

From the bottom of the **car park** where there is a low earth bank, cross over the bridleway, down the slope and turn left following the cliff edge. The slade (small dell or valley) in front of you leads down to the beach of Fox Hole which is named after the cave situated just across the valley below the cliff edge. The care home next to the car park, Heatherslade, was once the home of poet Vernon Watkins, a close friend of Dylan Thomas.

After around 200 metres, you will encounter another slade to **Fox Hole** beach. As you come around its head, take the small path along the cliff edge to a prominent headland, **High Tor**. There is a magnificent view to the west of the sweep of Oxwich Bay with the upland area of Cefn Bryn to the right. The impressive steep cliff just before the sand starts is Great Tor.

If you are feeling adventurous, it is possible to descend the steep slade to the west of High Tor to a path that runs east along the top of the lower cliff and scramble down to the largest bone cave in Gower, **Minchin Hole**. This is just visible by looking down to the left from High Tor where there is a large gash in the steep cliff slope.

From High Tor, carry on following the cliff top. Just below you at SS 5602 8682 is another famous cave, **Bacon Hole**.

MINCHIN HOLE

Minchin Hole, the largest bone cave in Gower

Minchin Hole is the largest and most impressive of all the Gower bone caves but is quite difficult to reach. The route down the cliff requires some very careful scrambling and access to the cave is not for the faint-hearted.

Extensive finds include the remains of a straight-tusked elephant, bison, soft-nosed rhinoceros, cave bear, reindeer, wolf and hyena showing that the cave was inhabited during the Upper Palaeolithic period. The later excavations by J Mason and JG Rutter proved that the cave was again inhabited during both the Romano-British period and again in the Dark Ages when the cave would have offered a secret hideout to anyone who made their home here. Finds of these periods include over 750 pieces of cooking pots, jars, beakers, dishes and bowls, spindle whorls, combs, finely-worked bone spoons, bronze brooches and numerous coins.

Keep following the cliff line around to where the path joins the road for a little while at **Hunts Farm**. Leave the road and drop to the head of the slade and climb out along a narrow path, keeping as close to the cliff edge as possible. At one point you will have to scramble over some uneven ground where there is a fort marked on the map. This is the site of an Iron Age promontory **fort**.

Continue on to **Pwlldu Head** from where a great vista unfolds to the east stretching from Pwlldu Bay, Caswell and across Swansea Bay to the Vale of Glamorgan, as far as Nash Point.

WALK 4 – PWLLDU HEAD AND BISHOPSTON VALLEY

BACON HOLE

Bacon Hole is one of Gower's larger and more famous bone caves with an entrance over 20m wide, extending for some 45m into the cliff at a good walking height. It was here in 1912 that Abbe Breuil and Professor Sollas discovered the 10 wide red coloured bands that gives the cave its famous name. These dark red streaks on the rock were sealed by a film of translucent calcite and were believed at that time to be rare examples of Palaeolithic art. For a while, Bacon Hole courted both notoriety and controversy but it was not long before it was noted that the celebrated marks changed with the passage of time and were nothing more than red oxide mineral seeping through the rock.

Excavations in 1850 by Colonel Wood revealed large numbers of animal bones dating to the Pleistocene era, such as narrow-nosed rhinoceros and straight-tusked elephant. Archaeological deposits were also discovered and comprised a thin dark layer with pottery assemblages indicating occupation from the early Iron Age to the medieval period. The cave is an important wintering site for two species of Horseshoe bat.

Down below is Graves End and **Pwlldu Cliffs Local Nature Reserve**. This reserve comprises a narrow strip of flat land on top of the cliffs and the slope down to the sea-washed rocks. Important habitats include limestone grassland and maritime cliffs and scrub. The area is managed using grazing to control the scrub and bracken.

Continue along the small path that drops down into the slade, marked by wooden posts and then climbs up to a swing gate. Keep climbing up some steps at the top of which is a fine view of Pwlldu Bay. Pass through a gate and cross the field to another swing gate. Continue on to another gate with a house on your left and turn right down a wide stony track signposted Pwlldu Bay. Ignore the first turning on the right which goes to a house.

Continue dropping to the right when you come to a gate to a house, ignoring the footpath sign to the left and this brings you to the houses at the back of the Bay. It is worth spending some time exploring the beach and shingle bank and reading about its industrial past and tales of smuggling (see Walks 2 and 3).

Follow the sign near the bridge that directs you to Bishopston Valley in a northerly direction (see Walk 3). Follow the stream up the valley until you reach some steps leading up to the left; there is an open space in front of you with the stream meandering away to the right.

WALKING ON GOWER

Ring of stones marking Graves End

Climb the steps and turn right when you join a path, signposted Kittle and Bishopston. This brings you back to the stream and a junction of paths. Turn left, leaving the stream valley at this point. Climb gently up this valley to a gate where you bear left, and few metres on turn right, following the sign to Southgate. The right fork leads to Highway Farm, famous for being the haunt of smugglers.

This brings you to a gate beyond which are some stone cottages at **Hael Farm**, which were used by smugglers in the 18th and 19th centuries. Go through the gate and follow the track that swings first left and then right. This brings you to another track at a bungalow where you turn left and onto Hael Lane. Follow this back to the start.

WALK 5

Pobbles, Three Cliffs Bay and Pennard Pill and Castle

Start/finish	National Trust car park, Southgate (SS 5540 8735)
Distance	6.5km (4 miles)
Total ascent	135m
Time	2hr
Refreshments	Three Cliffs Café, Pennard Stores, Post Office, Maddock's Tea Room in Southgate; Shepherds shop and café in Parkmill
Note	Care must be taken near cliff edges, especially in poor visibility or if children and dogs are in tow

This easy walk visits Three Cliffs Bay, considered by many to be the most beautiful beach in Gower, and then follows the picturesque Pennard Pill inland to the remains of Pennard Castle. A detour can be made if the tide is low enough to have a refreshing dip at the safer beach of Pobbles and to walk through the arch in the Three Cliffs. A woodland walk follows before returning across the golf links to Southgate where there are plenty of opportunities to buy an ice-cream or relax with a coffee.

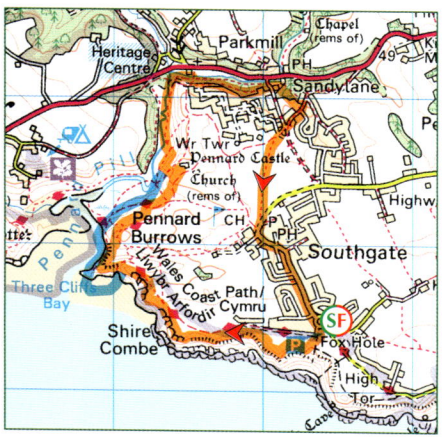

From the car park facing the sea, take the small path westward at the corner of the road that follows the cliff line. After about 50m you come to the top of a rocky outcrop. Beneath you is Foxhole Slade Cave that can be explored by dropping down to the left. The rocky cove has a lovely sandy beach at low tide. The headland to the east is High Tor beneath which is the impressive bone cave, Minchin Hole.

Three Cliffs at low tide from Shire Combe

WALK 5 – POBBLES, THREE CLIFFS BAY AND PENNARD PILL AND CASTLE

On a clear day to the south, the coast of North Devon and Hartland Point can be seen some 67km away, as well as Lundy Island to the right, in the distance.

Carry on along the small path that weaves its way through the gorse, following the cliff top until you reach another cove called Heatherslade. Soon you will be able to see the fantastic vista above Pobbles and Three Cliffs Bay (marked as Threecliff Bay on the 1:50,000 map), with the coast sweeping round to the impressive upright cliff of Great Tor, and Oxwich Bay beyond. Continue across open grassy areas, keeping the cliff top close on your left, and choosing paths that also stay near the edge for the best views of the limestone cliffs.

Ahead of you are the remains of **Pennard Castle** across the golf links, and the concrete water tower that was constructed in 1923 and decommissioned in 1986. It was built to provide water for the golf course after a drought in 1921–22 devastated the greens and fairways.

Check to see whether the tide is low enough to walk along the beach and around the headland of the Three Cliffs. The path now drops down the spine of a small ridge to the pebbly bank at Pobbles. Climb up the other side to gain the high point overlooking the first and highest of the three limestone spires that form Three Cliffs. Keep following paths high above Pennard Pill (down on your left), as close to the edge as possible, to Pennard Castle.

Pobbles Beach and Three Cliffs Bay at low tide from Shire Combe

Pennard Castle

PENNARD CASTLE

The first ringwork castle on this site was probably built by Henry de Beaumont, first earl of Warwick, when he was granted the lordship of Gower in the early 12th century. It had a bank and ditch around it with a primitive stone hall. On the opposite side of the valley, at Penmaen, there was a very similar castle of the same date. The only traces of this early castle are the footings of the hall at the west end of the courtyard, which was probably added to the ringwork in the early 13th century.

The castle was rebuilt in stone, probably by the de Braoses in the late 13th or early 14th century, using local limestone and reddish sandstone and the present-day ruins are the remains of this castle. In 1321 it passed to the de Mowbray family. It is an excellent location to find yellow whitlowgrass, a very rare alpine plant confined to this area of Britain. A small settlement grew up around the castle and to its east a solitary section of wall is all that is left of St Mary's Church, abandoned in 1532. Castle, village and church have all been overwhelmed by sand.

If the tide is low enough, walk across the sand and through the arch in the Three Cliffs. Turn right and walk upstream to the shingle bank, looking out for some boulders made of jagged stones of limestone of differing sizes cemented together.

The **boulders** are from a deposit called 'head', a type of breccia, which occurs frequently round the Gower coast. The angular fragments of rock were formed

Walk 5 – Pobbles, Three Cliffs Bay and Pennard Pill and Castle

during the last Ice Age by a process involving freeze–thaw action. They gradually moved down the slope due to gravity in a process called solifluction. The fragments were then cemented together with smaller fragments to form a breccia.

On the other side of the storm beach is an area of **salt marsh** that is inundated by spring tides. This is good area for birds such as little egret, heron and various species of duck.

Continue up the Pill making a short detour to see the remains of **Pennard Castle** where you rejoin the main route. Just after the boardwalk, a strandline of debris marks where the highest spring tides reach – a surprisingly long way up the valley.

Drop down from the castle and join the path that runs up the valley. The path climbs a little once it enters the woodland. Shortly afterwards you come to a sign; carry straight on heading towards the houses, ignoring the turning to the right to Southgate and a green metal bridge. If you wish to buy refreshments, cross the bridge to Shepherds shop and café on the other side. This is also an opportunity to visit the Gower Heritage Centre which is just along the minor road to the west.

Continue straight on where there is a sign for Coed Onnen, climb up the wooden steps and through the wood to a bend in the road. Cross straight over, turn right and climb the path through the woodland which is part of Kilvrough Manor Woods.

Turn right at the track and bear left at a triangular green area, ignoring other turnings on the left before this. Cross over the track to another track where you follow the right of way across the golf links towards the club house. Turn right onto the road and follow this through the village of **Southgate** back to the start.

The majestic limestone towers of Three Cliffs with the beach exposed at low tide

WALK 6

Three Cliffs Bay, Pennard Pill, Ilston Cwm and Bishopston Valley

Start/finish	National Trust car park, Southgate (SS 5540 8735)
Distance	17.5km (10.8 miles)
Total ascent	275m
Time	5hr
Refreshments	Three Cliffs Café and Pennard Stores; Shepherds shop and café at Parkmill; Beaufort Arms and shops in Kittle
Note	Care must be taken near cliff edges, especially in poor visibility or if children and dogs are in tow

An excellent day's walk that visits some of Gower's finest coastal landscapes and wooded valleys. Starting at the National Trust car park, where there are public toilets, the Three Cliffs Bay café and Pennard Stores, the route heads west along the cliffs to the stunning beaches at Pobbles and Three Cliffs Bay. It then swings inland following Pennard Pill and Ilston Cwm before returning back to the coast via Bishopston Valley to Pwlldu Bay.

From the **car park** facing the sea, take the small path westward at the corner of the road that follows the cliff line. After about 50m you come to the top of a rocky outcrop. Beneath you is Foxhole Slade Cave that can be explored by dropping down to the left. The rocky cove has a lovely sandy beach at low tide. The headland to the east is High Tor beneath which is the impressive bone cave, Minchin Hole.

View of Pennard Pill and Three Cliffs Bay from Pennard Castle

WALK 6 – THREE CLIFFS BAY, PENNARD PILL, ILSTON CWM AND BISHOPSTON VALLEY

Carry on along the small path that weaves its way through the gorse, following the cliff top until you reach another cove called Heatherslade. Soon you will be able to see the fantastic vista above Pobbles and **Three Cliffs Bay** with the coast sweeping around to the impressive upright cliff of Great Tor, and Oxwich Bay beyond. Continue across open grassy areas, keeping the cliff top close on your left, and choosing paths that also stay near the edge for the best views of the limestone cliffs.

Check to see whether the tide is low enough for you walk along the beach and around the headland of the Three Cliffs. The path now drops down the spine of a small ridge to the pebbly bank at Pobbles. If the tide is in, keep following the path along the cliffs, skirting around the edge of the golf links, and drop down into **Pennard Pill** where there is a pebbly storm ridge. If the tide is low enough, walk across the sand and through the arch in the Three Cliffs. Walk upstream to the shingle bank.

Continue up the Pill making a short detour to see the remains of **Pennard Castle**.

The path climbs a little once it enters the woodland. Shortly afterwards, you come to a sign; carry straight on heading towards the houses, ignoring the turning to the right to Southgate and a green metal bridge. To buy refreshments, cross the bridge to Shepherds shop and café on the other side. This is also an opportunity to visit the Gower Heritage Centre which is just along the minor road to the west.

Continue straight on where there is a sign for Coed Onnen, climb up the wooden steps and through the wood to a bend in the road. Cross straight over, down the track and over the bridge to the main road. Turn right along the main road and then left at the sign for Ilston 2km, just after the large stone building on the left which was once a school just before the Gower Inn. The woodland on the south side of the road is Kilvrough Manor Woods, a Wildlife Trust for South and West Wales Reserve.

At the end of the pub car park the path divides; take the left-hand fork that follows the stream bank. This then rejoins the other path at a bridge. Cross over and continue along the path that again stays close to the stream which meets the main path again at a bridge. Cross over this and on your right is the site of the Pre-reformation Chapel of **Trinity Well**.

> The **Chapel** ruins probably consist of the western portion of a small rectangular chapel, dating from the late Middle Ages and built, like many similar Catholic chapels, to honour the well and water supply. There is a strong tradition that John Myles used either this pre-Reformation chapel, or a small crude building erected next to it, as a Baptist meeting house between 1660 and 1663–4 after he was dismissed as minister of Ilston Church.

The stream appears and vanishes erratically along **Ilston Cwm** depending on how much rain there has been. This is because this valley crosses Carboniferous Limestone which is soluble in water and the water courses are underground.

Continue following the path by the side of the river. Do not cross the next bridge but continue along the right bank of the stream. Follow the path in the valley, crossing the stream a few more times until you arrive at **Ilston Church**.

ST ILLTYD'S CHURCH, ILSTON

Commemorative plaque for the site of the first Baptist church in Wales

The church stands on the site of an early Christian cell which was replaced by a wooden Celtic oratory, and soon after the Norman Conquest this was replaced with a stone church. In the 12th-century papal bulls, the site is mentioned as the church of St Cynwalon, but very little is known of this early Celtic saint. St Illtyd, however, is notable as the father of all Celtic saints in Wales. He was a contemporary of St Patrick and a pupil of St Germanus of Auxerre.

The present structure dates from the time of John de Breos, Lord of Gower, who presented it to the Knights Templar in the decade 1220–1230. Recent investigations have uncovered what could possibly have been a 'leper's window'. Notice the large yew tree on the right which is reputed to be over 600 years old.

St Illtyd's was established by John Myles on 1 October 1649 and was the first Baptist church in Wales. We know a great deal about the Baptist congregation of the time through the chance survival of the *Ilston Churchbook*, now preserved in America. Myles was rather disappointed that his first two converts at Ilston were women, though he consoled himself by believing that the Lord was 'thereby teaching us not to despise the day of small things'. The last baptism recorded in the Church book occurred in August 1660, a few months after the return of Charles II. By then, the Ilston Baptist church had a little over 250 members.

With the Restoration of Charles II to the throne, and the implementation of the Conventicle Act in 1664, Baptist services were declared 'dissenting assemblies'. Myles had no option but to gather up his flock and head for the safety of America. They settled in Massachusetts, at a town they called Swansea.

Graveyard and Ilston Church

Cross over the stream and turn right into the village and then cross the stream over a road bridge at Ilston Green. The route turns right here but 175m further up on your left is an old quarry, accessed from the road via a ford, which is now a wildlife reserve and is worth exploring.

The **Elizabeth and Rowe Harding Nature Reserve** can be accessed by making a short detour up the road. Cross a shallow ford on the left and pass over a stile but, if the stream is in spate, there is a footpath between the stream and Underwood House in the village. This Site of Special Scientific Interest was quarried for Carboniferous limestone until 1966.

The exposed stone face is of national geological interest, displaying an excellent cross-section through the Oxwich Head limestone, dating from the early Carboniferous Period. They consist of alternating beds of crinoidal limestone and clays associated with thin seams of coal, a geological exposure unique in Wales.

Follow the track past Rectory Cottage and then turn left just before the house and barns. The path then runs in a deep sunken lane, probably a very old route in the past, and then runs through fields and turns right to a farm. It then drops down to a track on the left and to a ford. Do not cross but take the path on the left and cross to a stile which takes the path into Moorlakes Wood. Follow this with the stream on your right until you come to a gate in the fence with private access

WALK 6 – THREE CLIFFS BAY, PENNARD PILL, ILSTON CWM AND BISHOPSTON VALLEY

signs on your left and right. Cross the fence and follow the path though a scrubby and sometimes boggy area until it comes to the perimeter fence of the aerodrome. Turn right and follow this towards the road, crossing over to take a track across the common which is open access, bear left at a fork and then turn left and follow along the hedge to Swn-y-Coed.

Take the path on the right just past the farm and follow the waymarked signs over fields to meet a stream at Brookside House. Follow the road across Barland Common to the B4436, turn left up the hill and cross over, taking the minor road immediately on the right that drops down to St Teilo's Church. Cross over the stream and follow the road to Kittle and to the green.

Pass between the houses leaving the National Trust sign on your left and follow the track to Great Kittle Farm. Take the path to the left of the entrance and follow this to where it divides and take the one that drops down the middle of the gulley, passing a fenced-off area where you will find a large limestone cavern.

Once you reach the bottom of **Bishopston Valley** (see Walk 3), which is normally surprisingly dry with no stream, turn right, signposted Pwlldu. If you wish to see the impressive swallow hole, turn left and walk for 250m.

> The **swallow hole** further up the valley is an impressive feature. The stream leading to it is only active during or after heavy rain, and even then the water often disappears just before it reaches the cliff edge where it would form a waterfall. Under exceptional circumstances, this enormous hole fills with water and the stream overflows down the valley.

Walking down the steep-sided valley, the stream-bed is very uneven, and after periods of heavy rain you will see water gradually starting to flow in the bed. When this changes character to being smoother you will see another dry stream course on your right, at the head of which is a cave called Guzzle Hole where you will be able to hear and see the underground stream. About 60m further down the valley, the path rises a little and there is a gated mine adit, the Long Ash Mine.

Continue down the valley, cross the dry stream-bed and just further along there is a resurgence where the water emerges from three underground passageways called sumps. Follow the path to Pwlldu Bay, ignoring two bridges that cross the stream and a side valley on the right. At a National Trust sign at **Pwlldu Bay** there is a bridge down to the left and a path climbing up the right. To explore the Bay, take the path that drops down to the bridge; do not cross, but head for the houses ahead. Pwlldu is full of historical and industrial interest (see Walks 2 and 3).

The route now takes the path that climbs out of the valley to the west. Turn left when you reach a track and follow the footpath which is signposted Pwlldu Head. This brings you on to the cliff top providing a wonderful vista to the east of Pwlldu

Bay and Caswell Bay. The coast sweeps away in the distance from industrial Port Talbot all the way to Nash Point in the Vale of Glamorgan, 40km away.

The path drops down the slope and then climbs up again to **Pwlldu Head**. Look down to your left to see **Graves End**, a ring of white stones that is the burial site of the dead of a ship called *The Caesar*. Head west along the cliff path to reach a waymarker, where on your left you can see two ramparts and ditches which were the defences for an Iron Age promontory fort.

Continue along the path near the cliff edge, around the slade that leads to Hunts Bay to the headland of **High Tor**. There is a magnificent view to the west of the sweep of Oxwich Bay with the upland area of Cefn Bryn to the right.

Minchin Hole, the largest bone cave in Gower (see Walk 4), is just visible by looking down to the left from High Tor where there is a large gash in the steep cliff slope. If you are feeling adventurous, it is possible to descend the steep slade to the west of High Tor to a path that runs east along the top of the lower cliff, and scramble down to the cave.

Carry on along the cliff top to **Fox Hole** where there is a cave just below the top of the cliff in the side of the slade opposite. Turn right to return to the start.

View east of Pwlldu Bay and Caswell Bay

WALK 7
Pennard Pill, Three Cliffs Bay and Parc le Breos

Start/finish	Parc le Breos estate car park (SS 5383 8963)
Distance	6.5km (4 miles)
Total ascent	125m
Time	2hr
Refreshments	Shepherds shop and café
Note	Part of this route along Pennard Pill is impassable if it is an extremely high-water spring tide

The first part of this walk explores the beautiful Pennard Pill and Three Cliffs Bay before climbing to the base of Cefn Bryn. A woodland walk through an old hunting estate follows where you will find the two archaeological gems of Cathole Cave and Parc Cwm long cairn.

From the car park walk back down the road, keeping right at the **Gower Heritage Centre**, and look out for the appearance of the stream on your left that has been flowing underground in the Carboniferous limestone up to this point.

Cross the main road and take the path into the wood. After a short distance, leave the main path and follow the signposted route to Three Cliffs Bay by taking the path on the left that follows the valley of **Pennard Pill**. Once you leave the woodland, look out for strandline debris by the path which indicates how high a spring tide can reach up this valley. The stone ruin on the left side of the valley is Pennard Castle (see Walk 5).

The salt marsh is a good place to spot a variety of birds including little egret, grey heron and various species of duck.

Where the stepping stones cross the stream, take the path climbing up across the hill slope to the right.

The **stepping stones**, which can be used to cross the small stream except during large spring tides, are thought to be the remains of a clapper-style bridge constructed by the Normans. This consisted of large flat slabs of stone supported by the stone piers that remain today.

Stepping stones across Pennard Pill

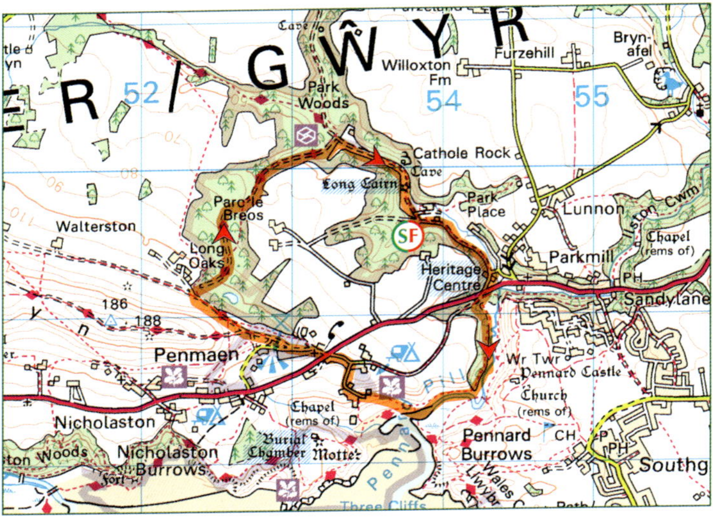

Continue straight on when you reach a track which becomes a tarmac road, and then left again at a T-junction and walk to the main road. Cross over and continue up the road to a cattle grid and a National Trust sign. Look back now and again for one of the best landscape views in Britain.

WALK 7 – PENNARD PILL, THREE CLIFFS BAY AND PARC LE BREOS

Ahead of you is Cefn Bryn (see Walk 8). Look out for boulders of Devonian conglomerate along the right side of the route just after you have crossed the main road. On your left is **Penmaen Church**.

Follow the road and then the track that leaves on the right when the road flattens out. Follow this, ignoring an obvious path that comes down the ridge ahead. You now join the Gower Way, at marker stone 12. Continue along the track and turn right through a swing gate into **Parc le Breos**. Follow the track through the woodland to a junction and to Green Cwm in **Park Woods** (see Walk 8). Small paths can be followed through the woodland down through the valley and these add interest, especially in spring when they have borders of wild garlic.

PARC LE BREOS

This is an excellent example of a 13th-century deer park. Established in the 1220s by John de Braose, Marcher Lord of Gower, it encompassed over 800 hectares, taking in the valleys of Green Cwm, Llethrid Cwm and Ilston Cwm. The introduced fallow deer shared the land with sheep or cattle and would have been hunted in the park by the Marcher Lord and his family and friends.

Wild garlic bordering one of the smaller paths through the woodland in Parc Cwm

CATHOLE CAVE

Interior of Cathole Cave where cave art was discovered in 2010

This natural limestone cave has a spacious chamber at its mouth and a small passage running 18m into the rock. It was first used in the Early Upper Palaeolithic period (36,000–25,000BC) as a temporary or transit camp. In the Late Upper Palaeolithic period (10,000–8000BC), after an intervening very cold phase, the cave was occupied more intensively. During the first excavation of the cave in 1864, finds were made only from the Mesolithic to medieval periods. A 1968 excavation by Aldhouse-Green revealed the earliest finds from the cave of two tanged points (a projectile point of flint or stone with a small projection at the base for attaching it to a wooden shaft) that may date to about 28,000 years ago, during an interglacial period during the Late Pleistocene. The engraving of a reindeer was discovered in 2010 on the wall at the back of the cave which has been dated to having been created at least 14,000 years ago. This is the oldest known rock art in Britain and possibly in north-western Europe. The entrance to the cave is now closed with a metal gate to protect the site.

Remains of red fox, arctic fox, brown bear, tundra vole and possibly reindeer were found at the same level as the Upper Palaeolithic tools, providing evidence of a cold climate about 12,000 years ago. Other animal remains excavated during the 19th century, which may predate the late glacial finds, include mammoth, woolly rhinoceros, red deer and giant deer. Several finds date to the Bronze Age, including a bronze socketed axe, two human skeletons and sherds of pottery from burial urns and other vessels.

WALK 7 – PENNARD PILL, THREE CLIFFS BAY AND PARC LE BREOS

PARC CWM LONG CAIRN

Neolithic Parc Cwm long cairn

Parc Cwm long cairn, also known as Parc le Breos burial chamber, was built around 5850 years ago during the early Neolithic. An excavation in 1869 revealed human bones belonging to at least 40 people, animal remains and Neolithic pottery. Samples from the site show that the tomb was in use for between 300 and 800 years, and that the humans buried there were hunter-gatherers or herders, not farmers.

Notice the absence of a stream running through the gorge. This is because the Llethrid Stream, which rises on Forest Common to the north, passes beneath the North Gower road and enters a swallow-hole, Llethrid Swallet, about 200m to the south, when it encounters the Carboniferous Limestone. It then passes underground beneath Llethrid Cwm and Green Cwm for a distance of 2km before emerging at Parkmill, or Wellhead.

Turn right, walking in the valley bottom until it swings around to the right. At this point, there is a path on the left (which is easily missed) that climbs the valley side. Then look for a side path to the right (also easily missed) that leads to a cave entrance with a metal grille.

Continue on to an open cave which is **Cathole Cave**. Return to the valley floor and continue down the valley where ahead is a large lime kiln on the left and Parc le Breos burial chamber on the right. Continue down the valley and back to the start.

WALK 8

Cefn Bryn, Broad Pool and Parc le Breos

Start/finish	Penmaen (SS 5314 8877)
Distance	13km (8.1 miles)
Total ascent	200m
Time	3hr 30min
Refreshments	None

The route follows the fine ridge of Cefn Bryn, the spine of Gower, to the impressive Arthur's Stone. There are superb views all along the ridge of north and south Gower with Three Cliffs Bay being the highlight. The picturesque nature reserve of Broad Pool is visited before exploring the beautiful parkland of Lodge Cwm. A short detour will allow you to marvel at Cathole Cave and the Parc Cwm long cairn. The return route is through the majestic woodland of Parc le Breos (see Walk 7). In 2010 an engraving was discovered inside a small niche northeast of the main gallery, around 10.5m from the cave entrance. This has been interpreted as possibly representing a deer. Uranium dating of calcite which overlays part of the engraving has been dated to approximately 12,500 BP giving a likely Upper Palaeolithic date for the figure.

CEFN BRYN AND TALBOT'S ROAD

Cefn Bryn is a five-mile-long ridge of common land, known locally as the backbone of Gower. One of the main attractions of the Bryn is a large Neolithic monument called Arthur's Stone not far from the summit of the ridge. There are also three Bronze Age burial cairns north-west of Arthur's Stone.

The route over Cefn Bryn is known as Talbot's Road, named after Christopher Rice Mansel Talbot, squire of Penrice Castle, who was a keen huntsman and would lead his hounds back to Penrice after hunting in the Parc le Breos estate.

From the car park, take the track up the hill to join the Gower Way. Follow this to a pile of stones from where you have a magnificent view of Three Cliffs Bay and the headlands, culminating in the stepped profile of Pwlldu Head. To the right

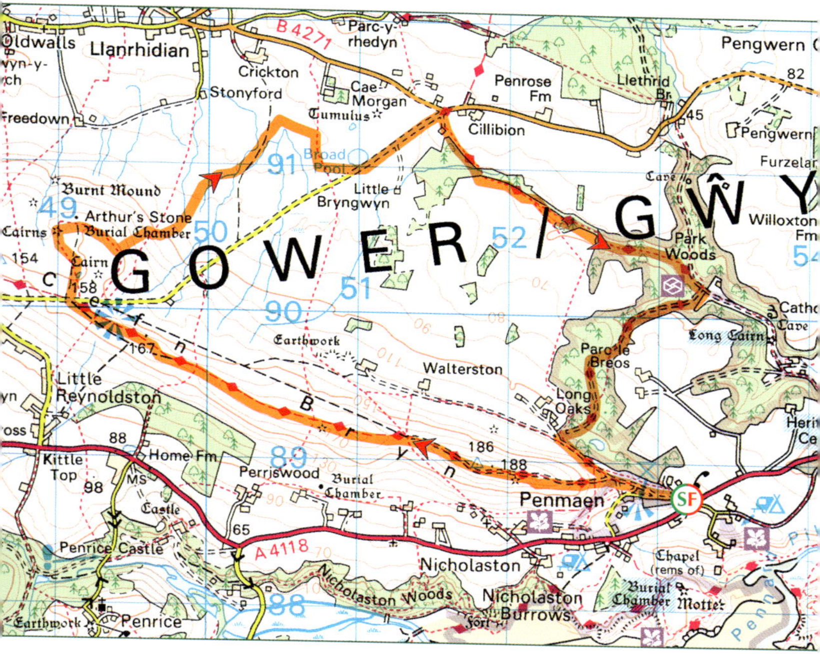

WALK 8 – CEFN BRYN, BROAD POOL AND PARC LE BREOS

View from Cefn Bryn across the common to Cilifor Top

The capstone and stone supports of Arthur's Stone/Maen Ceti, Cefn Bryn

is the sweep of Oxwich Bay leading to Oxwich Point. The large area of exposed stone is a cairn, one of around 60 piles of stones on Cefn Bryn. Some of these are Bronze Age while others were made by farmers clearing the fields.

Continue along the ridge of **Cefn Bryn** to the summit and then to the road. Cross the road and head north along the path, with a pool on your right. Continue left to the pile of stones, Great Carn, and then cross over to the large boulders of **Arthur's Stone** (see Walk 28). There is a fantastic view northwards of the Loughor Estuary, westwards of Llanmadoc Hill and north-eastwards of the South Wales coalfield and the Brecon Beacons beyond.

GREAT CARN

At 20m across, this is the largest cairn on Cefn Bryn and excavations have shown that underneath the pile of stones is a ring of boulders 12m in diameter. Traces of bone were found on a decayed plank within a stone setting and appears to be a burial. Further finds included a bedding, a pit, a posthole and a hearth together with sherds of Neolithic Peterborough ware pottery. This was in use when some of the Welsh chambered tombs were sealed for the last time.

Rushes line the edge of Broad Pool

BROAD POOL

Broad Pool is a large body of freshwater lying in a shallow basin on the limestone plateau beneath Cefn Bryn. It contains a rich assemblage of aquatic plants and is visited by a wide range of waterfowl and wetland birds including heron, snipe and little grebe together with passage migrants such as ruff and spotted redshank.

Facing north, take the path on the right that contours around the flat summit, ignoring the smaller path straight ahead. Broad Pool can be seen ahead over to your left, and further left again you can make out the sculpted ramparts of an Iron Age hill fort on the summit on Cilifor Top. Leave the path and head across the open moorland as best you can using pony tracks through the heather and gorse heath to **Broad Pool**. Continue along the road from the pool to the road junction; turn right down the track to the house and on to the Gower Way at marker stone 17.

Cross over the stile to the left of the house and follow the edge of Decoy Wood over a number of stiles with the impassable sunken track on your right. At a farm track turn right and cross the stream. Turn left once in the field and follow the fence on your left, still on the Gower Way, into the valley of Lodge Cwm. Look out for the limekiln on your left and a cliff of Carboniferous limestone behind.

WALKING ON GOWER

You may notice that the **stream** we were following earlier has disappeared with no evidence of surface water in the valley. It is now running underground in passageways in the Carboniferous limestone.

This track merges with one joining from the left and shortly after you come to a crossroads in Park Woods. It is really worth making a short detour by continuing straight on down the valley for 500m to see Cathole Cave and Parc Cwm Long Cairn (see Walk 7).

From the crossroads, turn right and follow the forestry track through **Parc le Breos** (see Walk 7). Pass through the swing gate, turn left and follow the track back to the start.

Path leading to Cathole Cave bordered by wild garlic (500m detour)

PARK WOODS

The woods have a great diversity of tree species including ash, sycamore, pedunculate oak, small-leaved lime and spindle. There is a spectacular display of wild flowers in the spring, and the woodland floor is carpeted in a mosaic of bluebells and ramsons. There are also a number of rare plant species including purple gromwell, herb paris and butcher's broom.

In 2010 the Forestry Commission started a four-year programme to restore the woodland to a more native state. This involves the cutting, chemical treatment and burning of rhododendron and cherry laurel, two invasive shrubs that shade out the ground and prevent native trees and ground flora from becoming established. The northern part is being managed as a coppice-type silvicultural system. Ash dieback is taking a terrible toll on Gower's ash woodlands.

WALK 9

Three Cliffs Bay, Tor Bay, Oxwich, Nicholaston Woods and Cefn Bryn

Start/finish	Penmaen (SS 5314 8877)
Distance	16.5km (10.2 miles)
Total ascent	290m
Time	4hr 30min
Refreshments	Oxwich Bay Hotel and cafés at beach car park

This route takes in some of the finest coastal scenery in Gower, with fantastic views of Pennard Pill, Pennard Castle, Three Cliffs Bay, Tor Bay and Oxwich Marsh and beach. The walk returns via the ridge of Cefn Bryn which gives panoramic vistas of the whole of Gower and beyond. Tor Bay is a beautiful sandy cove, an excellent place to stop for a swim and cool off on a hot summer's day.

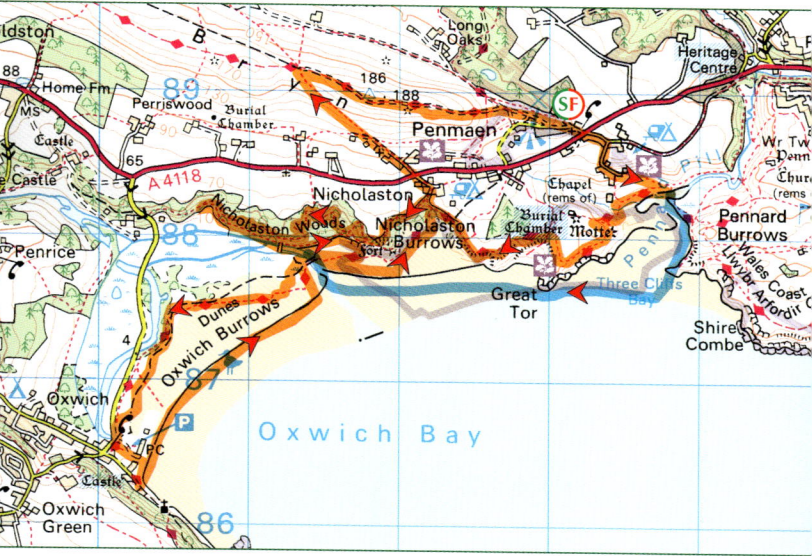

WALKING ON GOWER

Start at the car park at the beginning of the common near **Penmaen**. Cross back over the cattle grid and look out for boulders of Devonian conglomerate on the left just after the house.

> If you examine the surfaces of some of the flat faces of the rocks, you may notice polishing and parallel scratches. These are **slickensides** which are evidence that other rocks have moved against these surfaces during earth movements along the Cefn Bryn.

At the main road turn left and then first right, and right again at the sign for the beach, entering the National Trust property of Nott Hill. Over to your right as you walk down the hill is the headland of Oxwich Point.

Continue straight on after passing the gate at the end of the road and descend on the path across the slope down to the estuary of Pennard Pill.

Stepping stones across Pennard Pill with Pennard Castle in the background

WALK 9 – THREE CLIFFS BAY, TOR BAY, OXWICH, NICHOLASTON WOODS AND CEFN BRYN

The alternative route option leaves from here. It is possible to walk around Great Tor on the beach if there is a low spring tide. To do this, cross over the stepping stones, turn right, follow the stream and pass through the arch in the Three Cliffs. Turn right and ford the stream where it has separated into many channels and head for the base of Great Tor. Continue to the next stream and turn right to rejoin the main route at the footbridge.

Otherwise, do not cross the stepping stones but turn right to meet another path and then turn left.

At the bottom of the path, look left for a view of Pennard Castle (see Walk 5). The cliffs here are formed from Carboniferous limestone.

PENMAEN CASTLE

This was a small Norman timber ringwork, motte and bailey castle built in the 12th century, affording a stunning view of Three Cliffs Bay. At some point the wooden gate was destroyed by fire, either as a result of an attack or by accident. This was replaced by a drystone-walled gate tower that may have been Norman, or possibly rebuilt by Rhys Gryg ap Rhys, a Welsh lord who destroyed all the castles in Gower in 1217.

The **stepping stones** in the foreground are thought to be remains of a clapper-style bridge constructed by the Normans. This consisted of large flat slabs of stone supported by the stone piers that remain today.

Cross the small stream via the bridge and ascend the highest sand dune ahead looking for a path that leaves on the right. If your walk coincides with low water on a spring tide, it is possible to take an alternative route by heading west along the beach and rejoining the coast path at the headland to the west of Nicholaston Burrows.

The **dunes** were far more extensive and higher than they are today. Erosion from people walking and running on them is likely to have been the cause of their demise.

Turn right and follow the sandy path that climbs the slope to the top of the plateau and meets a path. Turn left here and follow the cliff path and, after a short distance, you will see an obvious ditch and earth rampart of the earliest Norman castle in Gower, Penmaen. The path brings you to the impressive headland of **Great Tor** where there is a magnificent view to the west of Tor Bay, the headland of Little Tor and Oxwich.

View west of Tor Bay and the cliffs of Little Tor from Great Tor

Keep following the cliff path that runs around the slade to a gate in the fence. Look back here for a fine coastal view; the furthest headland is Pwlldu Head and the one before is High Tor, with Shire Combe with Pobbles Bay just before. The view to the west is just as impressive with Nicholaston Burrows and Wood in the foreground and the beach and marsh of Oxwich National Nature Reserve beyond.

At the sign where a footpath joins from the right from Penmaen, carry straight on and do not drop down the slope. This enters the woodland and comes to a gulley where you continue on the path that runs along the top of the wood. You will ascend this path in the gulley later on. The route passes a **fort** marked on the map and then descends steeply to meet a path T-junction. Turn right and climb through the wood until you reach a path that joins on the left. Take this to return along the lower part of the wood with Oxwich Marsh down on your right. Continue to the end of the wetland and then turn right on to the Welsh Coast Path.

Follow the path that runs through the **dunes** to the car park near the end of the beach and to the Oxwich Bay Hotel. Turn around here and walk along the beach to the stream you crossed earlier. This may be fordable lower down the beach, otherwise cross over the **two bridges** further upstream. Continue on the path through the dunes and climb up the gulley to the point where you crossed earlier. Continue straight ahead, leaving the woodland and passing through a caravan park and bear left around the house to the main road. Cross straight over and climb past the houses to where a path leaves off to the right just past Nicholaston

WALK 9 – THREE CLIFFS BAY, TOR BAY, OXWICH, NICHOLASTON WOODS AND CEFN BRYN

House. On a clear day it is possible to see the north coast of Devon and Lundy Island to the south.

This path climbs to the ridge of **Cefn Bryn** where you turn right onto the main track, the Gower Way, this section of which is known as Talbot's Road (see Walk 8).

There are great **views** of the Brecon Beacons to the north-east, Swansea to the east, the Loughor Estuary with Llanelli across the water to the north and Pembrey Forest to the north-west. On this side of the estuary, you can make out the ramparts of the Iron Age fort on Cilifor Top beyond Broad Pool, and to the west is the vast expanse of the salt marsh ending in the spit of Whiteford Burrows with its distinctive conifer plantations.

Follow the track back to the start. Notice the large area of exposed stone which is a cairn, one of around 60 piles of stones on Cefn Bryn. Some of these are Bronze Age while others were made by farmers clearing the fields.

Crossing the bridge over the stream that drains Oxwich Marsh

WALKING ON GOWER

WALK 10

Millwood, Cefn Bryn, Reynoldston and Berry Wood

Start/finish	Millwood car park (SS 4931 8825)
Distance	10km (6.1 miles)
Total ascent	205m
Time	2hr 30min
Refreshments	King Arthur pub and post office in Reynoldston

This is a great route to choose in the Spring to see the woodland flowers in Millwood and Berry Wood, or to escape the crowds on the coast on a hot summer's day. The walk climbs up to Cefn Bryn and Arthur's Stone and then crosses the moor to Reynoldston and a chance for food and a pint at the King Arthur. It is downhill all the way through Berry Wood, a Wildlife Trust nature reserve and an excellent section through Millwood that visits the ponds before finishing at the old mill.

From the car park, go through the gate into Millwood. Turn right immediately along a footpath that climbs through the trees, ignoring a turning on the right which heads towards the wall. At the top of the wood, cross into the field and head slightly to the left to the stile on the horizon. Now aim just to the left of the mound called **Kittle Top** and to a stile in the fence in line with the trees ahead.

Pond in Millwood

Walk 10 – Millwood, Cefn Bryn, Reynoldston and Berry Wood

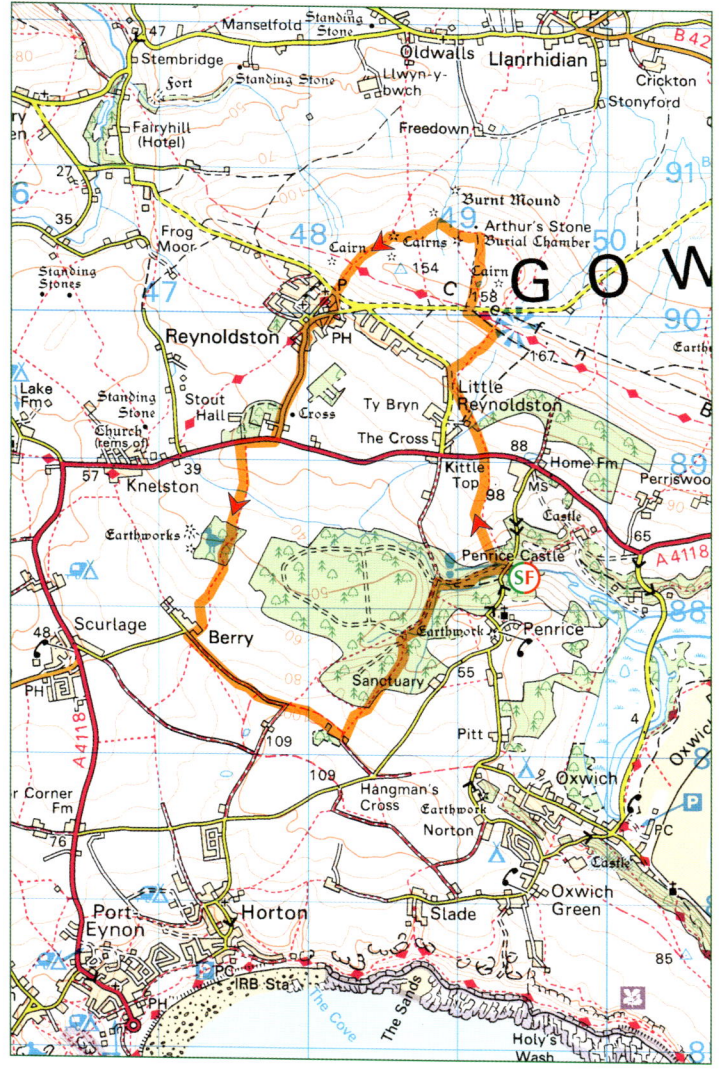

BERRY WOOD

Berry Wood Site of Special Scientific Interest

Berry Wood is an example of mixed woodland, rare in this part of Gower, situated on poorly drained glacial drift over millstone grit. Oak is present with birch, ash, hazel, sallow, rowan and aspen. The woodland structure suggests that the eastern half may have been clear-felled to provide timber during the Napoleonic Wars.

Cross over the main road and follow the fence on your left to a stile. Cross into the woodland and over another stile into open access land. Carry on with the fence on the left and turn right, in line with the house, along the path that climbs up the slope to the ridge of **Cefn Bryn** (see Walk 8). Just before the highest point, turn left on a path to the road. Looking back, you have a great view of Oxwich Bay, the Bristol Channel and the North Devon coast beyond.

Cross over the road and continue straight ahead to **Arthur's Stone** (see Walk 28) and then over to the pile of stones on the left which is the Great Cairn. Leave the cairn on the footpath in the north-west corner and join a path where you turn left. Head west and continue straight at a junction of paths. The path then swings to the left where you meet another crossing the moor. Turn left, now

The village green in Reynoldston

heading south-west, over to the ridge of Cefn Bryn and carry straight on the path to **Reynoldston** village.

Bear left coming down the hill with the post office in front of you and turn right down the track towards the King Arthur. Turn right at the road, pass the village green and church to reach the main road. Turn right and take the first footpath on the left. Cross straight over the field, following the old hedge line on your left to a stile. Cross over three more fields in the same direction and enter Berry Wood. Once in the wood, follow the yellow signs ignoring the ones for the permissive footpath.

Cross over the stile at the end of the wood and follow the hedge on your right to the next stile. Keep the hedge on your right until the slope levels out and then cross diagonally over the field to the stile in the far left corner with the last house of **Berry** on your right. Turn right onto the farm track and then left when you meet the bridleway. Follow this to a derelict stone building in line with the end of the woodland on your left, ignoring the track that joins from the right and the footpath that leaves on the left.

Turn left just after the stone ruin at Bryn-sil and follow the hedge to the stile on your right and cross this into **Millwood** (see Walk 11). There is a fine view of Tor Bay, Three Cliffs Bay and the stepped headland of Pwlldu Head.

Continue on the single-track path through the wood to join a main forestry track. Turn right immediately after to go down a path that joins the forestry track again at an impressive oak tree.

Turn right and take this to the ponds where you turn right and right again around the edge of the pond and follow the path along the stream back to the mill and the start.

WALK 11

Penrice Castle, Cefn Bryn, Three Cliffs Bay and Oxwich NNR

Start/finish	Millwood car park (SS 4931 8825)
Distance	20km (12.4 miles)
Total ascent	410m
Time	5hr 30min
Refreshments	Oxwich Bay Hotel, General Stores and cafés in Oxwich car park.

This is a varied walk that visits some of the finest features on Gower. The majestic Penrice Estate is first on the agenda followed by wonderful panoramic views from Cefn Bryn, before dropping down to the exquisite Pennard Pill and Three Cliffs Bay. The secluded Tor Bay and the impressive Great Tor cliff are encountered next, followed by an exploration of the wonderful wildlife found at Oxwich National Nature Reserve. The finale is a tour of Oxwich Point to the stunning beach of The Sands near Slade before returning via the tranquil woodland and ponds of Millwood.

The remains of the 13th-century Penrice Castle

WALK 11 – PENRICE CASTLE, CEFN BRYN, THREE CLIFFS BAY AND OXWICH NNR

From the car park at the entrance to **Millwood**, cross the stone stile to the right of the entrance gates and take the driveway up to the mansion, ignoring the Private sign on your left. Keep to the driveway which is the right of way through the estate, indicated with yellow markers. Pass between the derelict castle up to your left and the mansion on your right and follow the road as it swings round to the left.

MILLWOOD

Millwood is predominately a broadleaved woodland, covering 126ha, that was originally part of the Penrice estate. It still has the remnants of late 18th-century landscape tree planting within the original ancient trees. When it was an estate woodland, a variety of trees were planted, such as a row of lime trees and a glade of yews. Subsequent Forestry Commission plantings include western hemlock, Norway spruce, silver fir and beech, and the mixture of trees makes this an interesting area to explore and an excellent habitat for wildlife.

A diverse ash woodland field layer flourishes in the areas not heavily shaded by the conifers, including bluebells, ramsons, red campion, cow parsley, marsh marigold, meadowsweet and male fern. There is also an area of wild daffodil. The fauna present includes badgers, foxes, otters, buzzards, sparrowhawks and some bat species.

Fortunately, a four-year programme started in 2010 to restore the woodland to a native state. This involves the cutting, chemical treatment and burning of rhododendron and cherry laurel, two invasive shrubs that shade out the ground and prevent native trees and ground flora from becoming established. Western hemlock is being felled as it would regenerate readily if it was just thinned. Other conifer areas are being thinned to let more light in to promote the regeneration of native species.

Turn right after the red brick building and follow the yellow markers between the trees and over the field to the main road. Turn right, taking great care as this is very busy, and next left up to **Perriswood**. Turn right at the top of the road at the last house on the left. Cross the grassy area diagonally up to the left and take the path signed with a footpath arrow to a gate in the fence.

Continue straight on for 60m until you can turn right and pick up a footpath that diagonally traverses the slope through an area of gorse. Continue climbing steadily across the flank of **Cefn Bryn** from where there are excellent views of Penrice Castle and estate. On a clear day, it is possible to see the north coast of Devon and Lundy Island to the south.

WALK 11 – PENRICE CASTLE, CEFN BRYN, THREE CLIFFS BAY AND OXWICH NNR

PENRICE ESTATE

Walking through Penrice Estate in the autumn

The Penrice Estate is the oldest and largest of Gower's parklands and its origins can be traced to the 12th century when one of Henry de Beaumont's Norman knights was given the land after Henry had conquered Gower and founded the Marcher Lordship. The castle was originally made of wood; this was replaced by a stone building in the 13th century which still stands above the present house. This was abandoned in the 15th century when the Mansels built Oxwich Castle, the semi-fortified manor house closer to the sea. The four-storey neo-classical villa, built of Bath stone, was erected about 1775 by Thomas Mansel Talbot and designed by the architect Anthony Keck of King's Stanley, Gloucestershire.

This path climbs to the ridge of Cefn Bryn where you cross over the first path and turn right onto the main track, the Gower Way, this section of which is known as Talbot's Road (see Walk 8).

There are great **views** of the Brecon Beacons to the north-east, Swansea to the east, the Loughor Estuary with Llanelli across the water to the north and Pembrey Forest to the north-west. On this side of the estuary, you can make out the ramparts of the Iron Age fort on Cilifor Top beyond Broad Pool, and to the west is the vast expanse of the salt marsh ending in the spit of Whiteford Burrows with its distinctive conifer plantations.

Follow the track which then descends to the end of the common and cross over the cattle grid. Turn left at the main road and then first right and right again at the sign for the beach, entering the National Trust property of Nott Hill. Over to your right as you walk down the hill is the headland of Oxwich Point. Continue straight on after passing the gate at the end of road and descend the path across the slope down to the estuary of Pennard Pill.

The alternative route leaves from here. It is possible to walk around Great Tor on the beach if there is a low spring tide. To do this, cross over the stepping stones, turn right, follow the stream and pass through the arch in the Three Cliffs. Turn right and ford the stream where it has separated into many channels and

Three Cliffs Bay at low tide and the cliffs at Great Tor (alternative)

head for the base of Great Tor. Continue to the next stream and turn right to rejoin the main route at the footbridge.

Otherwise, do not cross the stepping stones but turn right to meet another path and then turn left. Cross the small stream via the bridge and ascend the highest sand dune ahead looking for a path that leaves on the right.

The **stepping stones** are thought to be remains of a 'clapper'-style bridge constructed by the Normans. This consisted of large flat slabs of stone supported by the stone piers that remain today.

Sand dunes in Oxwich NNR looking east

The fabulous Three Cliffs form the headland in the bay which sweeps around to Pennard Pill and the golf links.

At the bottom of the path, look left for a view of Pennard Castle (see Walk 5).

If your walk coincides with low water on a spring tide, it is possible to take an alternative route by heading west along the beach around Great Tor, rejoining the Coast Path at the headland to the west of Nicholaston Burrows.

Turn right and follow the sandy path that climbs the slope to the top of the plateau and meets a path. Turn left following the cliff path and, after a short distance, you will see an obvious ditch and earth rampart, the remains of Penmaen Castle (see Walk 9). The path brings you to the impressive headland of **Great Tor** where there is a magnificent view to the west of Tor Bay, the headland of Little Tor and Oxwich.

Keep following the cliff path that runs around the slade to a gate in the fence. Look back here for a fine coastal view with the furthest headland being Pwlldu Head and the one before is High Tor, with Shire Combe with Pobbles Bay just before. The view to the west is just as impressive with Nicholaston Burrows and Wood in the foreground and the beach and marsh of Oxwich National Nature Reserve beyond.

At the sign where a footpath joins from the right from Penmaen, take the path on the left that drops down to the sand dunes below. Follow the Coast Path markers through **Nicholaston Burrows**, over the bridges and through the dunes of **Oxwich NNR** (see Walk 12) to the end of the beach. Turn left at the road at the

WALK 11 – PENRICE CASTLE, CEFN BRYN, THREE CLIFFS BAY AND OXWICH NNR

top of the beach opposite the Oxwich Bay Hotel and take the path to **St Illtyd's Church** (see Walk 14). Continue along the path on the left and climb the steps through the wood. On your left is the site of a disused limestone quarry. You are now in the woodland section of Oxwich NNR.

Turn left at the top of the steps and follow the path to **Oxwich Point**. The path is forced away from the foreshore due to the extensive limestone quarrying along this part of the coast (see Walk 13). The path descends back down to near the sea again, providing a few opportunities to access the rocky platform and explore the limestone reef if the tide is out. The rock is made up of inclined layers of Carboniferous limestone that have been folded.

There is a fine view across to the north-east of Three Cliffs Bay and Pennard Castle.

Once around the Point, ignore the path that climbs up to the right signposted Oxwich Castle, and continue on the Coast Path. Just before this, look up on your right where you will see concrete buildings. These were part of the Chain Home Low radar site that detected shipping and low-flying aircraft in the Bristol Channel during World War 2.

This stretch of coastline is one of the finest in the UK and is unique in Gower with a grassy apron leading up to the cliffs a little inland. You can find many of the coastal bird species here such as stonechat, yellowhammer and even Dartford warbler.

The Carboniferous limestone reef is really impressive when it is exposed on low spring tides. **The Sands** is a delightful little cove that truly lives up to its simple name. This is a great place to take a refreshing dip and snorkelling over the reefs on either side will reveal a stunning underwater world.

Turn right just before The Sands to take the footpath up the valley, leaving the Coast Path, and join the road. Turn right at the T-junction at **Slade** and take the next bridleway on the left. Ignore the next bridleway on the right and footpath on the left and turn right just after a left-hand bend in the track. Follow the hedge on the left to the road and cross over on the bridleway to a ruined stone building at Bryn-sil. There is a fine view from here of Tor Bay, Three Cliffs Bay and the stepped headland of Pwlldu Head.

Turn right around the ruin and immediately left, over a stile, following the hedge to the stile on your right and cross this into **Millwood**. Continue on the single-track path through the wood to join a main forestry track. Turn right immediately after to go down a path that joins the forestry track again at an impressive oak tree.

Turn right and take this to the ponds where you turn right and right again around the edge of the pond and follow the path along the stream back to the mill and the start.

WALKING ON GOWER

WALK 12
Oxwich National Nature Reserve

Start/finish	Car park, Oxwich (SS 5029 8647)
Distance	4.5km (2.8 miles); with extension 10.5km (6.5 miles)
Total ascent	9m
Time	1hr; 2hr 30min with extension
Refreshments	Oxwich Bay Hotel and beach shops at Oxwich

This walk is based on the wildlife-rich Oxwich NNR which has many interesting features. A spring tide with low water around midday is an excellent time to do this route as you are then free to continue along the great expanse of sand for a further 2.5km. This extension takes in the stunning bays of Oxwich, Tor, Three Cliffs and Pobbles, together with the majestic limestone cliffs of Great Tor, Three Cliffs and Shire Combe. A detour along Pennard Pill to see Pennard Castle is also a memorable experience.

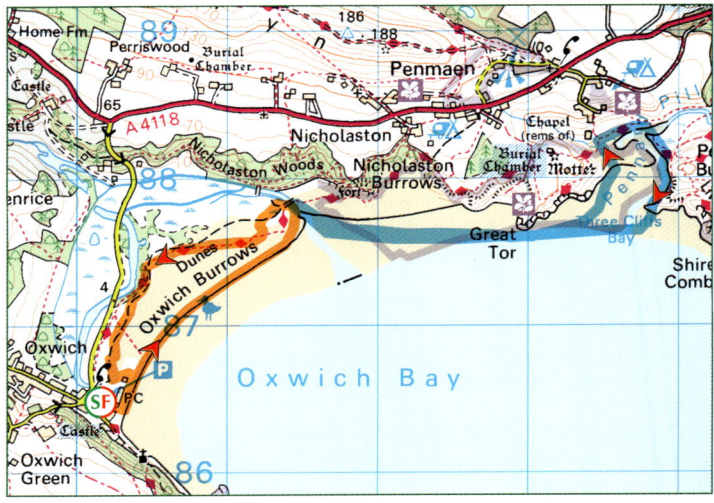

WALK 12 – OXWICH NATIONAL NATURE RESERVE

Crossing the bridge over the stream that drains Oxwich Marsh

Start on the **beach** in front of the car park. With the sea in front of you turn left along the strandline to the end of the car park and cross into the dunes; walk parallel to the beach to a nature reserve interpretation sign. Turn left on the footpath, pass through the swing gate and follow this through the dunes to where the stream meets the beach. There is a fine view of Penrice Estate and mansion (see Walk 11) up the valley and the village of Penrice with St Andrew's Church on the left (see Walk 14).

You can either return to the start of the walk along the beach (total of 4.5km) or continue over the bridge to Nicholaston Burrows, Tor Bay, Three Cliffs Bay and Pennard Pill and Castle (see Walk 5) and Pobbles Beach.

If the tide comes in to block the return along the beach, take the coastal foot path around Penmaen Burrows and gain the beach again at Tor Bay or Nicholaston Burrows.

OXWICH NATIONAL NATURE RESERVE

The dune areas are a great place to see wild orchids in late May and June. Like other coastal nature reserves in Wales, it has a high chalk content in its substrate because of the crushed shells in the sand which are blown inland from the bay. This means that many chalk-loving species, such as bee, early marsh, southern marsh and pyramidal orchids, can be found in relatively small areas. Butterflies associated with this habitat, such as dingy skipper and small and common blues, also occur.

The salt marsh contains sea-lavender, thrift and sea-purslane, with glasswort along the muddy creeks. The extensive reed beds are alive with birdsong in summer and contain nesting reed warbler, sedge warbler, grasshopper warbler and the nationally rare Cetti's warbler. Otters, herons and little egrets can be seen in the ditches and open water where they feed on the numerous fish that thrive here.

Aerial view of Oxwich Burrow, Marsh and Nicholaston Woods

The wooded cliffs of Nicholaston Woods are composed mainly of oak and ash, but also include wild service, wych elm and rock whitebeam. An impressive 600 species of plant have been recorded here, including stinking hellebore, dune gentian and round-leaved wintergreen. The woods are home to sparrowhawks, buzzards, woodpeckers and marsh and willow tits among others. There is a heronry in Penrice Wood and grey herons can often be seen flying backwards and forwards over the marsh.

Oxwich Bay originally only extended to the bottom of the limestone hills that flank the area, but several thousand years ago the bay began to extend when tidal forces created a barrier of sand dunes stretching across the bay. The lagoon that lay behind silted up, creating a salt marsh that remained, subject in the most part only to natural forces, until the 18th century.

In 1770, Thomas Mansel Talbot, the then owner of Penrice Estate, built an 8ft-high sea wall from the dunes to the north, preventing the sea from encroaching into the marsh. He then excavated a meandering ornamental lake running the length of the marsh and an extensive ditch system to drain away the freshwater flowing into the marsh from the numerous small streams and springs along the old cliff line. The land was gradually converted to rough pasture, dissected by drainage channels. The farming principle worked well, improving 200 acres of grazing land for sheep and cattle. However, maintenance of the drainage system, needed to prevent the pasture land from flooding, was neglected from sometime before World War 2. As a result the grazing animals had to be removed due to the rising water levels flooding the area. This in turn allowed aquatic plants such as common reed, yellow iris, and reedmace to gain control.

WALK 13

Oxwich Point

Start/finish	Car park, Oxwich (SS 5029 8647)
Distance	7.5km (4.6 miles)
Total ascent	155m
Time	2hr
Refreshments	Oxwich Bay Hotel and beach shop in Oxwich

The walk circumnavigates Oxwich Point with an opportunity to see some of the prettiest coastal scenery on Gower. The walk out to the Point passes the interesting church of St Illtyd and through a woodland section of Oxwich National Nature Reserve. The apron of land bordering the southern cliffs is unique on the peninsula and is a great area for spotting the numerous scrubland birds found in this habitat. The Sands is one of the most idyllic sandy coves one could find and an ideal place for a dip on a sunny day. The delightful fortified manor house of Oxwich Castle is the finale as the route descends back to Oxwich Beach.

Turn right out of the car park and walk along the beach to the Oxwich Bay Hotel. Turn left at the road and take the path to **St Illtyd's Church** (see Walk 14). Continue along the path on the left and climb the steps through the wood. On the left is the site of a disused limestone quarry and this is part of the woodland section of Oxwich NNR.

Turn left at the top of the steps and follow the path to **Oxwich Point**. The path is forced away from the foreshore due to the extensive quarrying along this part of the coast. The path descends back down to near the sea again, providing a few opportunities to access the rocky platform and explore the limestone reef if the tide is out. Notice how the rock is made up of inclined layers of Carboniferous limestone that have been folded.

There is a fine view across to the north-east of Three Cliffs Bay and Pennard Castle.

Once around the Point, ignore the path that climbs up to the right signposted Oxwich Castle, and continue on the Coast Path. Just before this, look up on your right where you will see concrete buildings. These were part of the Chain Home Low radar site that detected shipping and low-flying aircraft in the Bristol Channel during World War 2.

This stretch of **coastline** is one of the finest in the UK and is unique in Gower with a grassy apron leading up to the cliffs a little inland. Many of the coastal scrub bird species are found here such as stonechat, yellowhammer and even Dartford warbler. The Carboniferous limestone reef is really impressive when it is exposed on low spring tides. The Sands is a delightful little cove that truly lives up to its simple name. This is a great place to take a refreshing dip, and snorkelling over the reefs on either side will reveal a stunning underwater world.

The coast between Oxwich and Slade looking east

The Sands near Slade looking west

OXWICH LIMESTONE QUARRYING

Surprisingly large quantities of limestone were quarried from the coastline from the bay along to Oxwich Point. The cliffs are a mass of quarry faces and artificial scree slides. The blocks of limestone were formed into piles on the beach and small sailing ships would come alongside these at high tide to load their cargo.

The stone was exported across the Bristol Channel to north Devon and Cornwall where it was burnt to create lime which was then spread on the fields to reduce the acidity of the soil. The ships had to load igneous stone from the coast here to provide ballast for the journey back to Gower where they were dumped.

Turn right at **The Sands** and up the valley to the village of **Slade**. Turn right at the T-junction and continue up the road, passing through **Oxwich Green**. Bear right at a junction and down the hill, taking the turning to **Oxwich Castle** on the right.

OXWICH CASTLE

Oxwich Castle

It is very likely that there was an earlier castle on this site as a document refers to the *castrum de Oxenwych* in 1459, then owned by Philip Mansel. His grandson, Sir Rice, began work on the present house in the early 16th century. He gave his manor a mock-military gateway complete with the family's coat of arms carved in stone above the entrance leading to an enclosed courtyard.

His son, Sir Edward Mansel, created the much grander multi-storeyed range between 1520 and 1580. A long elegant gallery, a fashionable Elizabethan feature, was also added with panoramic sea views from its lofty position. The large top-storey windows were similar to those of Richmond Palace and Hampton Court. North of the castle is a ruined dovecote, probably contemporary with the early 16th-century buildings. It has a domed roof and a series of nesting holes in 11 layers and was a source of fresh eggs and meat. See Cadw's website for opening times and entrance fees https://cadw.gov.wales.

After visiting the Castle, take the right-of-way to the right of the grounds; this then turns left into the farmyard and then left again and down the hillside to the road. Turn right down the hill to the junction, turn right to the Oxwich Bay Hotel and across the beach back to the start.

WALK 14
Oxwich and Millwood

Start/finish	Millwood car park (SS 4931 8825)
Distance	13km (8.2 miles)
Total ascent	230m
Time	4hr
Refreshments	Oxwich Bay Hotel, General Stores and cafés in Oxwich car park

This walk combines a beautiful section of the south Gower coastline with the woodland part of Oxwich National Nature Reserve before crossing farmland to Millwood, an ancient woodland. There is plenty of history to discover with Penrice Church, Oxwich Castle and St Illtyd's Church. A mixture of coastal birds including stonechat may be encountered, as well as pond-loving species such as heron and kingfisher. The wetland areas in Millwood are excellent places to watch damselflies and dragonflies during the summer months. The remote sandy cove near Slade is one of the finest beaches to swim in the UK with the limestone reef providing endless rock-pooling fun.

From the car park, with the entrance gates to Penrice Castle on your left, follow the road that climbs up the hill. The majestic driveway leads to Penrice Estate (see Walk 11).

> The derelict stone building near the car park is the remains of a **16th-century corn mill** and there are two millstones leaning against the outer wall. The pond near the ruin is a quartered circular stew pond that was used to raise or hold fish, most likely carp, for consumption at the manor house.

On the way up the hill, turn left along a footpath to St Andrew's Church at **Penrice**. Pass around the church to the right, passing the impressive yew tree. With the church to your back, you have a good view of the village green and the pretty cottages.

WALKING ON GOWER

ST ANDREW'S CHURCH, PENRICE

This early 12th-century church dedicated to St Andrew was once owned by the Knights Hospitallers of St John of Jerusalem, but little of the original building remains today. A feature is the 'murder' gravestone to the left of the porch which is inscribed:

To the memory of Mary wife of James Kavanagh of Penmaen who was murdered by ------ on 3 October 1829 aged 75 years.

It is believed that the scratched-out name was intended to prompt the murderer to confess their sins. Whether this was successful is unknown.

WALK 14 – OXWICH AND MILLWOOD

St. Andrew's Church, Penrice

Penrice was once the principal village on Gower and once held four annual fairs and two weekly markets on the village green. The small stone here is known as the 'crying stone' as it was from here that the opening of the fairs and markets were announced. The earthwork marked on the map was once a Norman fortress and is a ringwork 30m wide with a raised oval platform protected by a ditch.

Turn left down the lane and cross over a stile with a fine view ahead of Nicholaston Burrows, the near vertical cliff of Great Tor and the majestic limestone headlands of Shire Combe, High Tor and Pwlldu Head. Beyond, on a clear day, is the Vale of Glamorgan coastline.

Turn right in front of the gate and down the hill. Cross over the next stile into the field and continue with the fence on your right. Look out for two lines of oak trees in the field, and at the second one leave the hedge and cross to a stile in the fence ahead. Cross over and turn left and follow the path through the woodland to where you meet a stream. Jump over this and turn right and over a stile into a field.

Follow the path, keeping the fence on your left, which brings you to an area of woodland and to the road in **Oxwich** village. Turn left. Look out for a thatched cottage on your left that was stayed in by John Wesley, one of the founders of the Methodist Church, in 1764.

WALKING ON GOWER

Oxwich Castle

Detour to visit Oxwich Castle
If you wish to explore Oxwich Castle, follow the blue alternative route by taking the next turning on your right, signposted Oxwich Green. This turns into a footpath that is sunken below two hedges and brings you to the road. Turn left and then right to **Oxwich Castle** (see Walk 13).

After visiting the Castle, take the right-of-way that is on the right of the grounds; this then turns left into the farmyard and then left again and down the hillside to the road. Turn right down the hill, passing a limekiln up on your right, and then left along the footpath into the woodland part of Oxwich National Nature Reserve where you rejoin the main route above **St Illtyd's Church**.

Main route continued
To continue without visiting the Castle, go straight on at the crossroads, passing the Oxwich Bay Hotel, and take the path to St Illtyd's Church. Continue along the path on the left and climb the steps through the wood. You are now

ST ILLTYD'S CHURCH, OXWICH

This ancient church is dedicated to Illtyd, a sixth-century saint who is reputed to have donated the stone font himself. A recess in the church, known locally as Doolamur's Hole, houses stone effigies of a knight and his lady made from sand particles cemented together with plaster and covered with a plaster coat. They are believed by locals to be members of the Norman De la Mare family who lived in Oxwich Castle and tragically drowned in Oxwich Bay in the 14th century. Another theory, due to the style of armour, is that they date from the 15th century and are of Sir John Penres and his wife, Margaret Fleming, who also owned Oxwich Castle. The Oxwich Bay Hotel was originally built as the Rectory for the church in 1788.

WALK 14 – OXWICH AND MILLWOOD

in the woodland section of Oxwich National Nature Reserve (see Walk 12). On your left is the site of a disused limestone quarry.

Turn left at the top of the steps and follow the path to **Oxwich Point**. The path is forced away from the foreshore due to the extensive limestone quarrying along this part of the coast (see Walk 13). The path descends back down to near the sea again where there are a few opportunities to access the rocky platform and explore the limestone reef if the tide is out. Notice how the rock is made up of inclined layers of Carboniferous limestone that have been folded.

Once around the Point, ignore the path that climbs up to the right signposted Oxwich Castle. Just

St Illtyd's Church, Oxwich

before the path, look up on your right where you will see concrete buildings. These were part of the Chain Home Low radar site that detected shipping and low-flying aircraft in the Bristol Channel during the World War 2.

This stretch of **coastline** is one of the finest in the UK and is unique in Gower with a grassy apron leading up to the cliffs a little inland. Many of the coastal scrub bird species are found here such as stonechat, yellowhammer and even Dartford warbler. The Carboniferous limestone reef is really impressive when it is exposed on low spring tides and The Sands is a delightful little cove that truly lives up to its simple name. This is a great place to take a refreshing dip, and snorkelling over the reefs on either side will reveal a stunning underwater world.

The Coast Path comes to a tarmac road at **Horton**. Turn right just after the first house and ascend the slade to meet a footpath. Turn left and cross the field, keeping the hedge on your right and then striking across to the far corner where the hedges funnel you to a track. Turn right and follow the path between the hedges to where it emerges into a field. Continue straight on with the hedge on your left and then cross the field when this comes to a corner. Head for the left of the trees

Oxwich Point

at Beggar's Pit and join a bridleway. Turn left to meet a road at **Hangman's Cross**. Cross straight over onto a bridleway which then meets another where you turn right. This comes to another bridleway where you turn right and then look for a stile in the hedge on your left about 30m further on. This can be quite easy to miss. Walk down this field keeping the hedge on the right.

Cross the stile at the corner of the wood, ignore the turn on the right, and carry straight on looking for a stile on the right. Enter **Millwood** and follow the path to a T-junction where you turn right. This comes to a main forestry track where you turn right and then immediately left. This soon joins the track again at an impressive oak tree where you turn right.

Follow this to the ponds where you turn right and right again around the edge of the pond and follow the path along the stream back to the mill and the start.

WALK 15
South Gower Cliffs and Port Eynon

Start/finish	Pilton Green (SS 4463 8713)
Distance	10.5km (6.5 miles)
Total ascent	140m
Time	3hr
Refreshments	The Ship Inn and shops in Port Eynon

This route explores the eastern section of South Gower Coast Nature Reserves and has some of the finest coastal scenery and wildlife in the UK. A good time to do this route is during low water during one of the largest spring tides of the year when the immense Carboniferous limestone wave-cut platform is exposed. Port Eynon Point is renowned as a seabird observatory throughout the year, and Culver Hole is an extraordinary feature well worth a visit.

Looking west at Foxhole Slade and the cliff with Paviland Cave at its base

Start at **Pilton Green** and, where the track joins the road, cross over the road to the left and follow the footpath sign through the gate into the field. Follow this to the coast path over the fields, keeping the hedge on your right, to arrive on the Wales Coast Path at **Foxhole Slade**. Turn left and follow the cliffs eastwards.

This stretch of coastline to Port Eynon has some of the finest **coastal scenery** in the UK and is part of the Gower Coast Nature Reserves. A variety of coastal birds will invariably be seen along the way.

The walk is made more interesting by taking detours to some of the headlands along the way to take in the incredible landscapes formed by the northerly dipping strata of the Carboniferous limestone. On the promontory on the opposite side of the slade are the remains of an Iron Age Fort and at its base is Goat's Hole, also known as Paviland Cave (see Walk 16), which is just hidden from view around the corner, facing out to sea.

The Coast Path drops down a slade and runs underneath **Overton Cliff** with superb views over Overton Mere, a huge expanse of limestone reef exposed during low spring tides, and Port Eynon Point. Ignore the path that climbs up to the left and follow the path around the head of **Overton Mere**, with the old quarries up

WALK 15 – SOUTH GOWER CLIFFS AND PORT EYNON

to the left. Continue along the lower path below the cliffs above rocks until it finishes and then scramble down to the right onto the limestone platform to see **Culver Hole**, which is tucked away in the cleft in the cliff on your left (see Walk 17).

Retrace your steps and take the first path that climbs up to the right to rejoin the Coast Path and continue to **Port Eynon Point**, an excellent place for looking over the Wildlife Trust Reserve and for watching seabirds. Drop down the waymarked route to the derelict building, the **Salt House**. An exploration of the intertidal area in front of the Point will be rewarded with a fine view of the dipping strata and Port Eynon Point Cave.

Culver Hole near Port Eynon Point

SALT HOUSE, PORT EYNON

The remains of two stone cottages and a number of stone-lined reservoirs are evidence of a salt house that commercially produced salt between 1550 and 1650. It was built for John Lucas and his wife in the mid 16th century by his father David.

Seawater was pumped from the cisterns to a panhouse, which was on an upper floor in the building, where it was evaporated in metal pans set over flues heated by a coal-fired furnace to leave salt. Salt was heavily taxed and subject to customs duties and the records show that it was illicitly produced and smuggled. The derelict stone buildings were domestic accommodation at the southern end while the more extensive ones to the north were workshops and stores.

The building was fortified in the 17th century with a series of musket loops in the wall of an extension, fuelling the legend of John Lucas' infamous career as a smuggler and pirate. The site was reputed to have had a secret passage as a means of escape, though there is no evidence of this. Salt production was abandoned in the 1870s and the buildings were later used as oyster fishermen's cottages.

The Salthouse, Port Eynon

Continue along the Coast Path following the waymarked route through the campsite to the roundabout by the shop. Turn left up the road and climb the hill through **Port Eynon**, noting the Ship Inn down a side turning on your right. Bear left at St Cattwg's Church and turn left down the road to Overton. Turn right almost immediately onto a footpath. Follow this across the fields and pass a wooded dell on the right.

ST CATTWG'S CHURCH

The original church was founded by St Cennydd, a missionary for St Cattwg the Wise of Llancarfan, in the sixth century, and in 1165 the church was given to the Knights of St John by Robert de le Mare. The current structure dates from 1861, though the font and a doorway are Norman, and there is an ancient piscina in the chancel.

Cross the stile and head across the field aiming for the left of Littlehills cottage. Ignore the track on the left of the gable end and turn left along the path to the derelict buildings at Hills. Pass to the left of the trig point in the field ahead and over a stile in the hedge. This path brings you to **Paviland Manor farm**. Follow the farm track north and then turn left over the stile and follow the ditch across the field to the hedge. Turn right to return to **Pilton Green**.

WALK 16
Thurba Head and South Gower Cliffs

Start/finish	Pilton Green (SS 4463 8713)
Distance	7km (4.5 miles)
Total ascent	45m
Time	2hr
Refreshments	None

This route explores the western section of Gower Coast Nature Reserves with some of the finest coastal scenery in the UK. Highlights include the cliffs around the Knave and the beautiful beach of Mewslade Bay. Several promontory Iron Age forts are encountered as well as numerous species of coastal birds including the iconic chough.

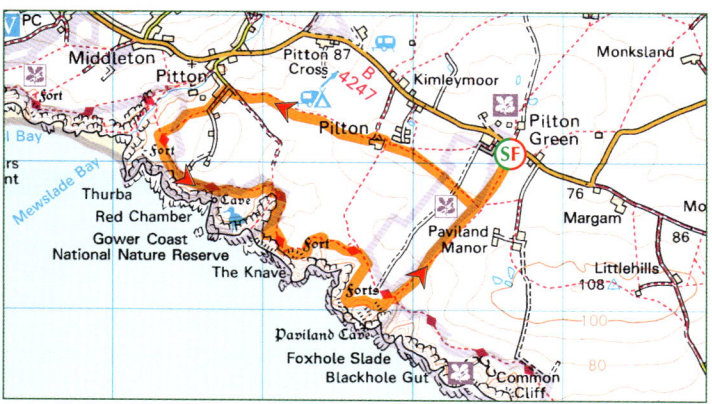

Start at **Pilton Green** and, from where the track joins the road, cross over and follow the footpath sign through the gate into the field. After crossing two fields turn right over the stile and follow the footpath, passing a pond on your right, to the farm at East Pilton and then West Pilton.

Take the path to the right of the second house to the farm track and turn left; at the Y-junction take the track to the right of the converted stone barn. Follow the sunken track keeping the hedge on your right. When this track finishes, carry straight on and across the field to the stile in the hedge. Cross over this field slightly to the right to another stile and then follow the yellow waymarkers through the small fields.

This comes to a footpath running between two hedges where you turn right to Great Pitton Farm. Follow the sign to the left between the farm buildings. Where this track swings around to the left, carry straight on along a grassy lane, ignoring the stile on your right. At the end of the drystone wall there is a sign to Port Eynon and a National Trust plaque indicating **Thurba Head**. Turn left and follow the cliffs eastwards. Lundy Island and the north Devon coast can be seen to the south on a clear day.

> This walk is made more interesting by taking detours to some of the **headlands** along the way to take in the incredible landscapes formed by the northerly dipping strata of the Carboniferous limestone. There are remains of Iron Age forts on five of these promontories. This is also a rich stretch of coastline for wildlife and bone caves, and the largest wave-cut platform (see Geology) of Carboniferous limestone in the world is nearly all exposed during the lowest spring tides of the year.
>
> The first headland worth exploring is Thurba Head just ahead. You can easily see the ramparts and ditches of the Iron Age fort when walking out to the point. The view west is of Mewslade Bay with Fall Bay behind; these become a single beautiful beach at low tide.

GOAT'S HOLE, PAVILAND

This is one of the most famous caves in the world for its astounding discovery of a nearly complete Upper Palaeolithic human skeleton, 'The Red Lady of Paviland'. The cave, with a pear-shaped entrance 10m high by 7m wide, was formed by the sea when sea levels were up to 8m higher than today. Within the chamber, daylight gleams from a fissure in the cave roof 20m above, just illuminating two hollows in the cave floor, the remnants of the two major excavations of the cave in 1823 and 1912.

It is difficult to access, either via an airy traverse across the cliff wall on the right of the slade looking out to sea or from the seaward side at low tide. This contrasts with the scene during the time the burial occurred when the cave overlooked a coastal plain rich in game animals.

The cave was first excavated in 1822, and the Reverend William Buckland, the first Professor of Geology at Oxford, re-excavated the cave the following year. It was during this secondary and more substantial exploration

Aerial view of Goat's Hole also known as Paviland Cave

that one of the world's most important archaeological finds was uncovered. At the time, however, the discovery was completely misidentified. Buckland was a devout Christian, and he did not recognise the full importance of his find as he believed that no human remains could be dated earlier than the Biblical Great Flood. Misguided by this preconception, his dating of the skeleton was drastically inaccurate.

Buckland discovered a whole side of an adult skeleton that had been covered with red ochre and buried with goods made from bone, antler and ivory. Perforated seashell necklaces also accompanied the body and it was largely these decorative items that led him to identify the skeleton as that of a female, probably a Roman prostitute or witch. This misidentification of the skeleton, plus the red staining of its bones by the red ochre that had been sprinkled over the body at the time of burial, gave Buckland's find the title of 'The Red Lady of Paviland'.

A further excavation of Goat's Hole, and a re-examination of the skeleton was made in 1912 which identified the 'Red Lady' as a male dating from the Upper Palaeolithic. The most recent radiocarbon analysis in 2009 indicates a date of 33,000 years ago, much older than previous estimates. In total, finds at Goat's Hole also include over 4000 worked flints, animal teeth, necklace bones, stone needles and mammoth-ivory bracelets.

Aerial view of The Knave and Deborah's Hole Nature Reserve looking west

Steeply inclined strata near Paviland cave looking east from Horse Cliff

The path rounds the head of a deep slade called Ram's Grove. Ignore a footpath that joins from the left. Leave the Coast Path to the right and make a detour along the cliff edge to discover the Knave Promontory Fort with the distinctive triangular cliff of **The Knave** separated from the main coastline. Continue to Horse Cliff, the next promontory to the east, where there is another fort, **Paviland** Promontory Fort. This affords a fantastic view back to The Knave. Look out for cormorants and shags on the rocks near the sea when the tide is in.

The cliff area bordering the inlet in front is a nature reserve named after a bone cave in the cliff, Deborah's Hole (see Walk 17).

You are forced back to the Coast Path at **Foxhole Slade**. This slade leads down to Goat's Hole, or Paviland Cave, a remarkable archaeological site. Turn left, leaving the coast, and follow the waymarked route across the fields and back to **Pilton Green**.

WALK 17

Rhossili Down, South Gower Cliffs and Port Eynon

Start/finish	Pitton Farm car park (SS 4268 8765)
Distance	20.5km (12.7 miles)
Total ascent	325m
Time	6hr
Refreshments	Shops, cafés and Worms Head Hotel in Rhossili; The Ship Inn and shops in Port Eynon

This stretch of coastline has some of the finest coastal scenery in the UK and is packed full of interest. The climb to Rhossili Down is rewarded with a superb panoramic view of Rhossili Bay and the majestic Worms Head. It is worth timing this walk with the largest spring tides of the year which expose the Carboniferous limestone reef at low water. Fall and Mewslade Bays are two of the finest coves in Gower and are inviting for a swim, depending on the time of year. Large winter storms throw some of the best surfing waves in the UK onto the reefs and you may see the spectacle of a surfer disappearing into the 'green room' in the notoriously hollow waves that break here.

From the car park in the farmer's field at **Pitton**, turn right back to the main road and cross over to the lane on the other side. Follow this up the hill, ignoring the footpath on the right. Take the next footpath on the left over a stile and this weaves its way around the back of the house to the end of a tarmac road. Cross over and take the stony track up the hill which takes you to the summit of **Rhossili Down** and the trig point. At 193m The Beacon is the highest point on Gower.

There are several Bronze Age burial cairns here built during the Early to Middle Bronze Age, 2500–1600BC.

There are impressive **views** from here on a clear day with Worms Head down to the left, and the patchwork of small fields that is The Viel (see Walk 21), a medieval field system that you will visit later. To the west is the south Pembrokeshire coastline and Caldey Island. If the visibility is really good, you can see Lundy Island just less than 50km away to the south and Hartland Point, the furthest western part of North Devon, some 64km away to the left of Lundy.

The trig point on the summit of The Beacon on Rhossili Down

SOUTH GOWER COAST NATURE RESERVES

Along the stretch of coast from Worms Head in the west to Port Eynon in the east, the numerous nature reserves are collectively known as the South Gower Coast Nature Reserves. Deborah's Hole, Long Hole Cliff, Overton Mere, Port Eynon Point and Sedgers Bank are owned by the National Trust and managed by the Wildlife Trust for South and West Wales. Worms Head and the cliff areas around Fall Bay and Mewslade Bay comprise the Gower Coast National Nature Reserve.

Limestone grassland develops on thin soils where lime-loving flowering plants thrive, such as the purple wild thyme, the delicate yellow hoary rock-rose, the yellow goldilocks aster and the blue spring squill. Coastal grassland develops on soils affected by salt-spray, where you will find beautiful clumps of thrift, the gentian-blue spears of spiked speedwell and the leafy, pink-flowered stems of the small restharrow. Coastal heath characterised by heather (ling), bell heather and western gorse is found on pockets of deeper soils which are generally in sheltered locations and on the cliff tops, where you will also find the vibrant small yellow flowers of tormentil and clusters of yellow lady's bedstraw.

The maritime cliff, ledge and crevice plant communities have developed all along the length of the coastline on the steep limestone cliffs, from the high-water mark up to the cliff tops in pockets of soil that have accumulated in cliff crevices. Plants found here include thrift, sea campion, rock sea-spurrey and golden and rock samphires.

WALK 17 – RHOSSILI DOWN, SOUTH GOWER CLIFFS AND PORT EYNON

The habitat mosaic supports a rich and beautiful population of flowering plants, six of which are nationally important: hoary rock-rose, goldilocks aster, spiked speedwell, small restharrow, yellow whitlowgrass and nit-grass. Hoary rock-rose is scarce throughout the UK but thrives here and its delicate bright yellow flowers can be seen dotted across the cliffs. Similarly, yellow whitlowgrass has a threatened status, with Gower being the only recorded site for this species in Britain with the largest colonies found between Mew Slade valley and Paviland. Despite the name, this plant is not a grass but it is a small flowering plant that usually grows in crevices on the cliff faces.

Rhossili Down is an old beach level that was subsequently eroded by ice sheets during the penultimate Ice Age. The Bay has developed as the rocks that form its arms are harder Carboniferous limestone, whereas the softer Old Red Sandstone rock lying between is less resistant to attack by Atlantic storms.

The platform underneath Rhossili Down is a solifluction terrace (see Walk 22). The lone house was once the Rectory for the churches at Rhossili and Llangennith and is now rented out by the National Trust (see Walk 18).

Turn left at the trig point and descend in the direction of Rhossili Village and Worms Head. Turn right just before the church in **Rhossili** and follow the path around the graveyard to join the road.

There is a memorial in the church to **Petty Officer Evans** who was born in Middleton and perished with Scott in the Antarctic in 1912.

Walking down to Rhossili from The Beacon on Rhossili Down

WALKING ON GOWER

Carry on down the road through the village and past the Worms Head Hotel. Pass through the gate opposite the National Trust shop and look right for a great view of Rhossili Beach and Down. The route is made more interesting by walking on the grassy platform above the cliffs from where the Iron Age fort and quarried cliff faces below can be seen.

The Gower Way path brings you to the hut that was once a Victorian coastguard lookout and is now staffed by Coastwatch. Ahead of you, at low tide, is the causeway to **Worms Head** (see Walk 19). This area is the Gower Coast National Nature Reserve, just one of a series of reserves along the cliffs to the east.

From the hut, follow the cliffs to the east to **Tears Point** and along the Coast Path above **Fall Bay**. If the tide is low and the sand is exposed, you can descend to the beach and cross to the corner of Fall Bay and ascend the slade back to the Coast Path, or even continue beneath the cliffs to Mewslade Bay and rejoin the route at the limestone outcrop with a cave in Mew Slade valley.

The Coast Path stays on the high part of the cliff as the lower path is now impassable due to cliff erosion. The area on your left is the medieval field system of The Viel.

Take the right fork and follow the cliff path along the cliffs. This rejoins the path that has been running along the wall. Turn right and then take the next path on the right to drop down to Mew Slade. Once in the valley bottom, cross over the stone wall in front of a limestone outcrop with a cave. Pass to the right at its base and up the slope on the Coast Path to the corner of the drystone wall.

The first headland worth exploring is **Thurba Head** just ahead. You can easily see the ramparts and ditches of the Iron Age fort when walking out to the point. The view west is of Mewslade Bay and Fall Bay, which become a single beautiful beach at low tide. Lundy Island and the north Devon coast can be seen to the south on a clear day.

The path rounds the head of a deep slade called Ram's Grove. Ignore the footpath that joins from the left. Leave the coast path to the right and make a detour along the cliff edge to discover the Knave Promontory Fort with the distinctive triangular cliff of **The Knave** separated from the main coastline.

A fantastic view looking west of this is from Horse Cliff, the next promontory to the east where there is another fort, **Paviland** Promontory Fort. Look out for cormorants and shags on the rocks near the sea when the tide is in.

The cliff area bordering the inlet in front is a nature reserve named after a bone cave in the cliff, Deborah's Hole.

Continue around **Foxhole Slade** to the point where there is a fine view of the cliffs on the western side of the valley and the ramparts of the fort. Goat's Hole cave (see Walk 16) is hidden from view just around the corner from Foxhole Slade on its western side in the lower cliff.

WALK 17 – RHOSSILI DOWN, SOUTH GOWER CLIFFS AND PORT EYNON

DEBORAH'S HOLE NATURE RESERVE

Deborah's Hole is named after a small bone cave located on the eastern side of The Knave. The reserve has been partially surface quarried for limestone, either as building stone for walls or for burning to produce lime for agricultural fields. This has left a broken surface and varied soil depth which has not allowed subsequent agricultural improvement, as has occurred on the cliff top of Horse Cliff, immediately to the east.

Later, the Coast Path drops down a slade and runs underneath **Overton Cliff** with superb views to the east of Overton Mere, a huge expanse of limestone reef exposed during low spring tides, and Port Eynon Point. Ignore the path that climbs up to the left and follow the path around the head of **Overton Mere**, with the old quarries up to the left. Continue along the lower path below the cliffs above the rocks until it finishes and scramble down to the right onto the limestone platform. Culver Hole is tucked away in the cleft in the cliff on your left. An exploration of the intertidal area in front of the Point will be rewarded with a fine view of the dipping strata and Port Eynon Point Cave.

Retrace your steps and take the first path that climbs up to the right and joins the Coast Path again and take this to Port Eynon Point, an excellent place for looking over the Wildlife Trust Reserve and for watching seabirds. Drop down the waymarked route to the derelict building, the Salt House (see Walk 15). Continue

Low tide at Overton Mere exposing the wave cut rock platform

along the Coast Path following the waymarked route through the camp site to the roundabout by the shop.

Turn left up the road and climb the hill, noting the Ship Inn down a side turning on your right. Bear left at St Cattwg's Church (see Walk 15) and turn left down to the road to Overton. Turn right almost immediately onto a footpath. Follow this across the fields and pass a wooded dell on the right. Cross the stile and head across the field aiming for the left of **Littlehills** cottage.

Ignore the track on the left of the gable end and turn left, heading in the same direction, along the path to the derelict buildings at Hills. Pass to the right of the trig point in the field ahead and over a stile in the hedge. This path brings you to **Paviland Manor farm** where you follow the farm track north and then turn left over the stile and follow the ditch across the field to the hedge.

Turn left and then turn right, over a stile and across the field with the hedge on your right to a stile. Continue in the same direction on the footpath through the fields, passing a pond on your right to the farm at **East Pilton**. Take the path to the right of the house at West Pilton to the farm track where you turn left and, at the Y-junction, take the track to the right of the converted stone barn. Follow the sunken track keeping the hedge on your right.

CULVER HOLE, PORT EYNON

Culver Hole is located in a very tall natural cleft just above the high water mark. It has been walled up to protect a number of floors and slippery stairways, and this 18m-high masonry wall is pierced with a number of rectangular and oval windows. The inner face has hundreds of L-shaped nest holes and it is thought to have been a colombarium where pigeons were bred for food for people living in Port Eynon Castle on the cliff top above, first referred to in lawsuit records in 1353.

The word 'culver' has been traced to Middle English terminology, derived from the Old English *culufre*, meaning pigeon or dove, and culverhouse is still used in some parts of Britain for a dovecote. The cave has been excavated in the past and archaeological artefacts were found. During an investigation in December 1989, a small fragment of an antler was found trapped in an alcove.

When this track finishes, carry straight on across the field to the stile in the hedge. Cross over this field slightly to the right to another stile and then follow the yellow waymarkers through the small fields. This comes to a footpath running between two hedges where you turn right to Great Pitton Farm. Continue straight on, ignoring the footpath on your left, to join the road and return to **Pitton**.

Culver Hole near Port Eynon Point

WALK 18

Rhossili Down and Bay, Fall Bay and Mewslade Bay

Start/finish	Pitton Farm car park (SS 4268 8765)
Distance	12km (7.4 miles)
Total ascent	250m
Time	3hr 30min
Refreshments	Café and shops in Rhossili

From the summit of Rhossili Down there are superb panoramic views of Gower, numerous burial cairns and two Neolithic burial chambers. A lofty traverse of the ridge is made before dropping down to the impressive 4.7km of uninterrupted sand of Rhossili Bay. You can catch your breath with a stop in Rhossili and an opportunity to have something to eat and drink. Next is a flat walk out to the Lookout with an option to extend your walk, if tides and time allow, to explore Worms Head. The return is via the idyllic beaches of Fall Bay and Mewslade Bay.

From the car park in the farmer's field at **Pitton**, turn right back to the main road and cross over to the lane on the other side. Follow this up the hill, ignoring the footpath on the right. Take the next footpath on the left over a stile and this weaves its way around the back of the house to the end of a tarmac road. Cross over and take the stony track up the hill which takes you to the summit of **Rhossili Down** and the trig point. The Beacon is the highest point on Gower at 193m.

There are several Bronze Age burial cairns here built during the Early to Middle Bronze Age, 2500–1600BC.

There are impressive **views** from here on a clear day with Worms Head down to the left and the patchwork of small fields which is The Viel (see Walk 21), a medieval field system that you will visit later. To the west is the south Pembrokeshire coastline and Caldey Island. If the visibility is really good, you can see Lundy Island just less than 50km away to the south and Hartland Point, the furthest western part of North Devon, some 64km away to the left of Lundy.

Rhossili Down is an old beach level that was subsequently eroded by ice sheets during the penultimate Ice Age. The Bay has developed as the rocks

WALK 18 – RHOSSILI DOWN AND BAY, FALL BAY AND MEWSLADE BAY

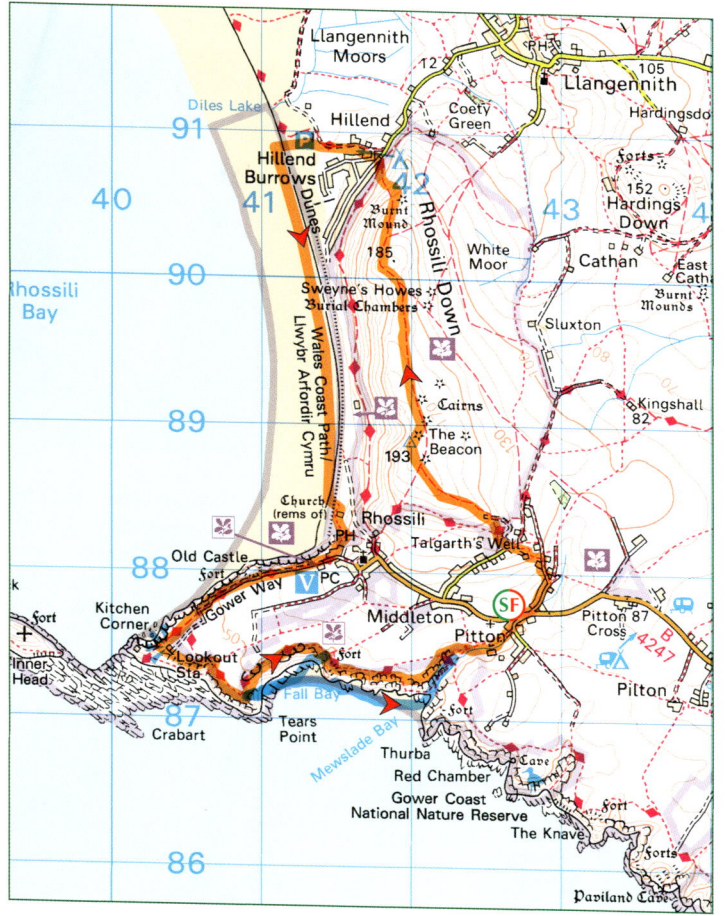

that form its arms are harder Carboniferous limestone, whereas the softer Old Red Sandstone lying in the middle is less resistant to attack by Atlantic storms.

The platform underneath Rhossili Down is a solifluction terrace (see Walk 22). The lone house was once the Rectory for the churches at Rhossili and Llangennith and is now rented out by the National Trust.

Ponies grazing the cliff top near Old Castle fort

Drop down the hill from the trig point and, just after the path joins from the right, there is an obvious circle of stones marking the site of a burial cairn (see Walk 22). The boulders here comprise rounded quartz pebbles in sedimentary rocks formed during the Devonian period (see 'Geology' in the Introduction). Looking to the east you can see the ridge of Cefn Bryn and stepped sea cliff of Pwlldu Head.

Take the right hand fork when the path divides and, if you wish, descend the slope down to the right to visit the burial chambers of **Sweyne's Howes** (see Walk

Northern burial chamber of Sweyne's Howes on Rhossili Down

21). Climb back up to the ridge, from where you can see below the remains of the Chain Home Low radar site that detected shipping and low-flying aircraft in the Bristol Channel during World War 2. Drop down the front of the Down towards the campsite at **Hillend**, go through the gate and turn left through the caravan park to the beach.

RHOSSILI RECTORY

Rhossili Down and the Old Rectory on the solifluction terrace

The house at the base of Rhossili Down is the Old Rectory and is referred to in 1720. Its location roughly midway between Llangennith and Rhossili is because the rector originally ministered at both churches. By the end of the 18th century it was in disrepair but was rebuilt in the 1850s and bought by the National Trust in 1995. It can be rented as a holiday cottage and has one of the highest occupancy rates for a National Trust property in the UK.

However, the building has a reputation for being haunted. In the depths of winter something very unpleasant comes out of the sea and into the house and others have reported suddenly finding themselves in a pool of cold air in a corridor and hearing a voice whispering, 'Why don't you turn round and look at me?' The ghost of the Reverend John Ponsonby Lucas, who served the two villages between 1855 and 1898, is said to gallop his horse along the sands between Llangennith and Rhossili.

THE HELVETIA

The wooden remains of the Helvetia shipwreck on Rhossili beach

On the evening of 31 October 1887, the *Helvetia* was driven by strong south-easterly winds across the infamous Helwick sandbank off south-west Gower, losing a substantial part of her deck cargo of wood in the process. Fortunately the crew were able to keep the ship from further damage and she rode the waves around Worms Head and into the relative shelter of Rhossili Bay. They dropped anchor to wait for the weather to improve and the captain went ashore, along with the local coastguard, believing that all was well.

Unfortunately, a few hours later the wind suddenly changed direction to the west and strengthened, ripping the anchor free of the sands and driving the *Helvetia* perilously close to the expansive sands of Rhossili beach. The order was given to abandon ship and all of the crew made it safely ashore. The next day the sands of Rhossili were strewn with the remains of her timber cargo and the ship was stranded where she lies today. The wood was quickly gathered and sold on to local merchants, while the *Helvetia* was unceremoniously stripped of anything of value.

The **strandline** has a varied collection of seashells, giving a clue to the species that live in this high-energy sandy beach which faces due west and bears the brunt of huge Atlantic rollers during storms. They include oyster, razor shell, prickly cockle, sand gaper and carpet shells, although the oysters may be

WALK 18 – RHOSSILI DOWN AND BAY, FALL BAY AND MEWSLADE BAY

remnants from the large oyster fishery based in Port Eynon in the past. The area of sand to your right where the stream crosses the beach at Diles Lake is believed to be the location of the wreck of the Dollar Ship (see Walk 20).

Turn left once you reach the sand and walk down the bay to the steps below **Rhossili**. Just before you come to the steep cliffs, you may see the oak ribs of the wreck of the *Helvetia* if the tide is low enough. Climb the steps up to the village and turn right past the Worms Head Hotel and on to the cliff path.

Pass through the gate opposite the National Trust shop where there is a board showing the tide times. Make a note of the tide times if you wish to extend the walk by crossing over to Worms Head. The route is made more interesting by walking on the grassy platform above the cliffs from where you can see the Iron Age fort and quarried cliff faces below.

The Coast Path brings you to the hut that was once a Victorian coastguard lookout and is now run by Coastwatch. The officers here may also be able to advise you on tide times for crossing the causeway. Ahead of you, at low tide, is the causeway to Worms Head and the walk can be extended as described in Walk 20.

From the hut, follow the cliffs to the east to **Tears Point** and along the Coast Path above Fall Bay. If the tide is low and there is sand exposed, you can descend to the beach and cross to the corner of Fall Bay and ascend the slade back to the Coast Path or even continue beneath the cliffs to Mewslade Bay and rejoin the route at the limestone outcrop with the cave in Mew Slade valley. Follow **Mew Slade** valley back to the start in **Pitton**.

Looking west towards Fall Bay

WALK 19

Rhossili, Fall Bay and Mewslade Bay with Worms Head option

Start/finish	St Mary's Church Rhossili car park (SS 4167 8807), or National Trust car park opposite Worms Head Hotel
Distance	5.5km (3.3 miles); with extension 10km (6 miles)
Total ascent	60m; with extension 135m
Time	1hr 30min; with extension 3hr
Refreshments	Café, pub and shops in Rhossili
Note	There is room for a few cars in Rhossili Church car park but this is likely to be full during the summer; there is alternative parking (National Trust) at the end of the road.

This route may be short in distance but is packed full of interest and breathtaking scenery. An extension out to Worms Head over the tidal causeway is an experience not be missed but be careful to check the tides to avoid being marooned, a fate that befell the famous Welsh poet Dylan Thomas. The bays of Mewslade and Fall are simply stunning and the intertidal reef of Crabart offers rich marine wildlife in the multitude of rock pools carved in the limestone.

There is a memorial in the church to **Petty Officer Evans** who was born in Middleton and perished with Scott in the Antarctic in 1912.

Turn left from the church car park in **Rhossili** and left again to walk around the church to join the road. Bear right and down the road through the village, past the Worms Head Hotel. Pass through the gate opposite the National Trust shop where there is a board showing the tide times. Make a note of these if you wish to extend the walk by crossing over to Worms Head. The route is more interesting if you walk on the grassy platform above the cliffs from where you can see the Iron Age fort and quarried cliff faces below.

The Coast Path brings you to the hut that was once a Victorian coastguard lookout and is now staffed by Coastwatch. The officers here may be able to advise you on tide times for crossing the causeway. Ahead of you, at low tide, is the causeway to **Worms Head**.

WALK 19 – RHOSSILI, FALL BAY AND MEWSLADE BAY WITH WORMS HEAD OPTION

RHOSSILI QUARRIES

The cliffs in between the village and the Coastguard Lookout Station have been worked in the past for the limestone which was a valuable export. It was taken across the Bristol Channel to Devon and Cornwall to be burned and turned into lime to fertilise the acid soil there. On the cliffs below, just above water level, you may find iron rings and the signs of a quay built to load the extracted limestone from the quarries, which scar the cliffs, onto waiting boats.

Extension – Exploring Worms Head

The causeway is only exposed for 2.5 hours before and after low tide. It is a fairly easy 15min crossing over uneven ground to the Inner Head, and taking a route over to the left provides an easier time over the rocks. Ascend the path over the Inner Head and descend at its end down to the start of Low Neck. The traverse to the Middle Head is a different experience as it involves a short scramble over difficult terrain.

Once over this rocky section to the Middle Head, join the path on a grassy section and then over a limestone arch called the **Devil's Bridge**. A short rocky section brings you to the Outer Head where you can scramble up to the summit of the Outer Head, passing a prehistoric midden on the way. Retrace your steps back to the start of the Inner head where you can take the path that skirts around its base back to the start of the causeway. Under no circumstances should an attempt be made to wade or swim back across the causeway. Dylan Thomas visited the Worm and was cut off by the rising tide (see Walk 21). Once across, turn right on the lower grassy slopes and follow the path to climb via a slade to rejoin the main

Devil's Bridge on Worms Head

route. There are excellent panoramic views to the west of Caldey Island and the south Pembrokeshire coast and to the east of the cliffs along south Gower.

> Look out for a narrow vertical slit in the bare limestone on the slope up to your right on the way to the end of the Outer Head. This is a vent for a **blowhole** and air can be heard, and felt, rushing out. During extremely large Atlantic swells the blowhole is a spectacular sight from the mainland, when water can be seen shooting hundreds of feet into the air.

Main route continued

From the hut, follow the cliffs to the east to **Tears Point** and along the Coast Path above **Fall Bay**. If the tide is low, and there is sand exposed, you can descend to the beach and cross to the corner of Fall Bay and ascend the slade back to the Coast Path, or even continue beneath the cliffs to Mewslade Bay and rejoin the route at the limestone outcrop in Mew Slade valley.

The Coast Path stays on the high part of the cliff as the lower path is now impassable due to cliff erosion. The area on your left is called The Viel, a medieval field system (see Walk 21).

At a 90-degree bend in the stone wall, take the right fork and follow the cliff path above the cliffs. This rejoins the path that has been running along the wall where you turn right and then take the next path on the left, ignoring any on the right that drop into the valley below, to the main road at **Middleton**.

Take the next footpath on the left down the track and turn right off the track at the next footpath through The Viel. Turn off right at the next footpath which takes you to back to the start at **Rhossili church**.

WORMS HEAD CAUSEWAY

Anchor on Worms Head causeway

The causeway is in the middle of an upward fold in the rocks caused by the major fault. This is shaped like the hull of an upturned boat and is termed a pericline as it dips down at both ends. On the left of the causeway, the beds of limestone slope inland at 30–45 degrees at first; suddenly there is a gap in them and then they continue, but now sloping out to sea. The rocks here are full of small faults filled with thick bands of white calcite that are easy to find. They are minor side faults to a much larger fault that runs along the south Gower coast. All these faults have weakened the rock strata, causing them to be eroded and weathered at a faster rate than the rocks of the mainland and Worms Head.

There is a 2m-long ship's anchor embedded in the rocks near the start of the causeway. It is all that remains of a wrecked ship whose cargo of coal kept the local households warm for many a year after it ran aground.

The causeway is one of the best places in Glamorgan for wintering purple sandpipers and black redstarts. Seals are resident on the Worm, and gannets are regularly seen offshore.

WORMS HEAD

The causeway at low tide leading out to Worms Head

Worms Head, made of Carboniferous limestone, is shaped like a giant sea-serpent that really lives up to its Viking name *wurm*, meaning a limbless dragon. It comprises the Inner, Middle and Outer Heads, separated from the mainland by a vast tidal causeway. The faint remains of a promontory Iron Age fort can be traced on the summit area of the Inner Head. The single line of defence can be seen as an outward facing scarp up to 4m wide and 1m high running in a semi-circle along the sloping southern side of the head, the northern side being defended by naturally steep cliffs. It is markedly different from most of the promontory forts on Gower, and Cadw considers it of national importance as an unusual type of prehistoric or early historic enclosure. The top of the Inner Head is perfectly flat, indicating that it was once a wave-cut platform (see Geology).

The rectangular enclosure at the beginning of the Inner Head is thought to be the remains of a medieval farm building. Sheep were kept on the Inner Head until recently and Swansea University erected two rectangular enclosures to exclude them in order to ascertain the effect they were having on cropping the grass. The grass inside is significantly longer and in thicker mats than that outside. The grasses on the Middle Head, where sheep are absent, are also much denser.

The extensive limestone reef exposed at low tide is an excellent habitat for edible crab and lobster and it was divided up between the Rhossili locals, the richest grounds being allocated to the senior men in the village.

WALK 20
Rhossili Down, Llanmadoc Hill and Broughton Burrows

Start/finish	St Mary's Church Rhossili car park (SS 4167 8807), or National Trust car park opposite Worms Head Hotel
Distance	16km (9.9 miles)
Total ascent	380m
Time	4hr 30min
Refreshments	Café and shops in Rhossili; Kings Head pub in Llangennith
Note	There is room for a few cars in Rhossili Church car park but this is likely to be full during the summer; there is alternative parking (National Trust) at the end of the road

A good day's walk ascends Rhossili Down, from where there are superb views in all directions, and where there is plenty of evidence of past use with stone cairns and the burial chambers of Sweyne's Howes. Further majestic panoramas unfold from the summit of Llanmadoc Hill before the descent to the dunes at Broughton Burrows and the return along the 4.5km sandy beach of Rhossili Bay via Burry Holms.

Looking towards Worms Head from the trig point on The Beacon

131

Walking on Gower

WALK 20 – RHOSSILI DOWN, LLANMADOC HILL AND BROUGHTON BURROWS

There is a memorial in the church to **Petty Officer Evans** who was born in Middleton and perished with Scott in the Antarctic in 1912.

From the church in **Rhossili** turn left, following the sign for the Coast Path and then turn right, heading for Rhossili Down, ignoring the turning on the left; go through the gate onto National Trust land.

Climb to the The Beacon, marked by a trig point on the summit of **Rhossili Down**, which rises to 193m, and look back for a fantastic view of Worms Head and the south Pembrokeshire coastline, with Caldey Island further to the west on a clear day. If the visibility is really good you can see Lundy Island just less than 50km away to the south, and the furthest part of North Devon, Hartland Point, some 64km away to the left of Lundy.

Rhossili Down is an old beach level that was subsequently eroded by ice sheets during the penultimate Ice Age. The Bay has developed as the rocks that form its arms are harder Carboniferous limestone, whereas the softer Old Red Sandstone lying in the middle is less resistant to attack by Atlantic storms.

Drop down the hill from the trig point and, just after the path joins from the right, there is an obvious circle of stones marking the site of a burial cairn (see Walk 22). The boulders here comprise rounded quartz pebbles in sedimentary

Looking north along Rhossili Down to Llangennith Beach

rock formed during the Devonian period (see Geology). Looking to the east you can see the ridge of Cefn Bryn and stepped sea cliff of Pwlldu Head.

> The platform underneath Rhossili Down is a **solifluction terrace** (see Walk 22). The lone house was once the **Rectory** for the churches at Rhossili and Llangennith and is now rented out by the National Trust (see Walk 18).

Take the right-hand fork when the path divides and, if you wish, descend the slope down to your right to visit the burial chambers of **Sweyne's Howes** (see Walk 21). Climb back up to the ridge and drop down the front of the Down towards the campsite but turn right before the gate and take the path with the fence on your left. Turn left just after the house, cross over the stile into the field and pass through two fields with the fence on your left.

Cross the bridge over the stream, turn right and over the road leading to a house. Turn left after the swing gate, walk up past the paddocks and turn right, and over the stile in the corner of the field. Keep the fence on your left and follow the path to the road. Turn left and walk up the hill to the T-junction in **Llangennith**, with St Cenydd's Church on your right.

Turn right and follow the road, passing the Kings Head, and bear left at the bend onto a footpath and over a stile into a field. Cross this to another stile, over the track and over the stile in the hill fence. Turn right on the path and then cross over another under the power lines. Down on the right is Tankeylake Moor that is reputed to have been the site of a bloody battle between two local clans.

Shortly after, this meets another footpath where you turn right, walking parallel with the power lines. Turn left when this meets a track and follow this up to the summit of Llanmadoc Hill and turn right to the trig point. There is an excellent

TANKEYLAKE MOOR

There is a local legend that this was the site of a ferocious battle between the occupants of the fort on Hardings Down and those living at the Bulwark fort on Llanmadoc Hill. Tonkin, who was the leader of the Bulwark clan, was killed and so much blood was spilled that it flowed over his boots, giving rise to the name Tonkin's (Tankey) Lake. You may be able to see several mounds; these are the remains of land clearance cairns made by people during the Bronze Age when they first cleared the area for cultivation.

panorama from the summit: to the north are the Loughor Estuary and Burry Inlet; and the South Wales coalfield to the north-east.

The sand dunes covered in marram grass at Llangennith Burrows

Follow the crest of the hill to meet a track coming up from the right; turn left and drop down the hillside. Ahead of you is the long spit of Whiteford Burrows National Nature Reserve.

Go straight on across a bridleway and then bear left when the path forks to join a footpath that runs along the hill fence, where you turn left.

Continue along the fence, ignoring a path on the right, to where there is a stile which you cross and continue with the fence on your left. At **Delvid** turn right through the gate and then left in front of the stone building, ignoring the sign to Llangennith and Broughton. Continue straight on to join the Wales Coast Path where you turn left and follow the signs to Rhossili, passing the caravan park on your left, to **Twlc Point**. The path runs around the edge of Broughton and Llangennith Burrows to Spaniard Rocks and Burry Holms. It is possible to explore the island when the tide is out where you will find the remains of an Iron Age fort.

It is worth dropping down on the east side of **Bluepool Corner** to see the large circular natural rock pool, around 5m in diameter and roughly the same depth, just down to the left.

In 1800 a fisherman called John Richard found a quantity of gold *moidores*, **Portuguese gold coins**, and doubloons among the rocks here. Others have found coins, including divers searching the seabed.

On the opposite side of the bay is a sea arch called the Three Chimneys, and just around the corner to the south-west is **Culver Hole** in which the remains of 41 bodies have been excavated, dating to the Middle Bronze Age, 1450–1000BC. Other finds included Early Iron Age pottery, a late Celtic female figurine, coins and brooches from the second century AD and a ninth-century brooch.

Drop down to the beach and cross the bay to the steps below **Rhossili**.

The **strandline** has an interesting collection of seashells, giving a clue to the species that live in this high-energy sandy beach which faces due west and bears the brunt of huge Atlantic rollers during storms. They include oyster, razor shell, prickly cockle, sand gaper and carpet shells, although the oysters may be remnants from the large oyster fishery based in Port Eynon in the past. Keep an eye out for where a stream crosses the beach at Diles Lake where you may discover treasure from the infamous Dollar Ship.

THE DOLLAR SHIP

A local legend tells of a Spanish vessel carrying part of Catherine of Braganza's marriage dowry, possibly 400,000 silver coins, to Charles II of England in the mid 17th century. She was caught in a storm and shipwrecked, possibly lured ashore by wreckers, and dashed on to the sand where she broke up. Tradition has it that the bulk of her cargo was salvaged by Mr Mansel of Henlly of Llandewi, a notorious local smuggler and possibly the wrecker of the ship. By the time others could approach safely, most of the silver had gone and so had Mansel, having fled or possibly been murdered.

In 1807 William Bevan and others discovered a mass of silver dollars and half-dollars opposite Diles Lake during an exceptionally low tide. They desperately collected as many coins as they could before the tide came in, Bevan using his trousers to carry the booty by tying up the ends of the legs. More than 12lbs of silver dollars and half-dollars were collected. They had been minted in Peru, and were dated 1625 and 1639 and stamped with the head of Phillip IV of Spain.

Coins were not seen again until 1833, when a severe storm removed sand from the beach revealing coins, two cannons, cannon balls, musket balls and an astrolabe. A mini Klondike-style gold rush ensued with many fights breaking out on the beach, and thousands of coins were lost again to the sand as the tide engulfed the powerless men.

Just before you reach the steep cliffs, you may see the oak ribs of the wreck of the *Helvetia* if the tide is low enough (see Walk 18). Climb up the steps and turn left to walk through **Rhossili** back to the church.

WALK 21

Gower Coast NNR, Rhossili Down and Hardings Down

Start/finish	Pilton Green (SS 4463 8713)
Distance	19.5km (12 miles)
Total ascent	380m
Time	5hr 30min
Refreshments	Cafés and Worms Head Hotel in Rhossili; Kings Head in Llangennith

This classic Gower walk along a stretch of coastline has some of the finest coastal scenery in the UK. Fall and Mewslade Bays are two idyllic coves that are inviting for a swim, depending on the time of year. The climb to Rhossili Down is rewarded with superb panoramic views of Rhossili Bay and the majestic Worms Head. It is worth timing this walk with the largest spring tides of the year which reveal the exposed Carboniferous limestone reef at low water. After a welcome break for refreshment at the Kings Head in Llangennith, the return route is over the hill fort on Hardings Down and cross country back to Pilton Green.

From **Pilton Green**, where the track joins the road, cross over the road to the left and follow the footpath sign through the gate into the field. Follow this over the fields to the Coast Path, keeping the hedge on your right. When you reach the Wales Coast Path at **Foxhole Slade**, turn right and follow the cliffs westwards. This slade leads to Goat's Hole, also known as Paviland Cave, a remarkable archaeological site (see Walk 16).

This walk is made more interesting by taking detours to some of the **headlands** along the way to take in the incredible landscapes formed by the northerly dipping strata of the Carboniferous limestone. There are remains of Iron Age Forts on five of these promontories. This is also a rich stretch of coastline for wildlife and bone caves, and the largest wave-cut platform of Carboniferous limestone in the world that is nearly all exposed during the lowest spring tides of the year (see Geology).

Walking out to the first headland to the right of Foxhole Slade, cross the ramparts and ditches of **Paviland** Iron Age promontory fort. Cross over to the top

WALKING ON GOWER

WALK 21 – GOWER COAST NNR, RHOSSILI DOWN AND HARDINGS DOWN

of Horse Cliff from where there is a fantastic view of the distinctive triangular cliff of the Knave, separated from the main coastline, and the inlet of Deborah's Hole, named after the bone cave in the cliff (see Walk 17). Look out for cormorants and shags on the rocks near the sea on The Knave when the tide is in.

Continue west around Deborah's Hole crossing **The Knave** promontory fort on the headland. The path rounds the head of a deep slade called Ram's Grove. Ignore the footpath that joins from the right and continue west to where there is a National Trust sign for **Thurba Head**. You can easily see the ramparts and ditches of the Iron Age fort when walking out to the point.

Entrance to Goat's Hole, the burial site of the "Red Lady of Paviland"

THE VIEL

The headland between Worms Head and the villages of Rhossili and Middleton contains a medieval strip field system known as The Viel, or The Vile, an old Gower dialect name for a field. This is a rare surviving feature and is of national importance. The narrow fields are still communally farmed and are enclosed by drystone walls near the cliffs and earthen banks inland. Within these boundaries the unenclosed strips are divided further by narrow unploughed ridges known as landshares.

The **view west** is of Mewslade Bay in front of you and Fall Bay further on which become a single beautiful beach on a low spring tide. Lundy Island and the north Devon coast can be seen to the south on a clear day. Keep a lookout for the many different birds that live in this coastal habitat.

Follow the Coast Path arrows and drop down the slope into the valley of Mew Slade and cross over the wall.

The Knave looking east from the Iron Age cliff fort

There is an alternative route which is possible if the tide is low enough with a continuous stretch of sand from Mewslade Bay to Fall Bay. If you wish to take this option, turn left and descend the valley and scramble down to Mewslade Bay. Cross in front of the cliffs looking for an impressive sea cave and then on to the far end of Fall Bay. Scramble up the rocks and climb the slope to rejoin the main route at Tears Point.

Otherwise, turn right and then left up the valley side to meet a footpath. Turn left and then left again, now ignoring the Coast Path sign. The path runs around the top of the cliff to rejoin the Coast Path by the drystone wall which marks the boundary of a medieval field system called The Viel.

Continue around the head of **Fall Bay**, dropping down the slade to the beach if the tide is out and if you wish to explore this interesting area, rejoining the route at Tears Point. The two tiers of steep cliffs on the left are popular with rock climbers and offer some spectacular routes.

The path comes to **Tears Point** where the Coast Path swings right to the Lookout Station which was once a Victorian coastguard base and is now staffed by Coastwatch. There is a fine view of the causeway and Worms Head from here (see Walk 19).

Walk 21 – Gower Coast NNR, Rhossili Down and Hardings Down

DYLAN THOMAS, RHOSSILI

Rhossili was a favourite destination for writer Dylan Thomas who, as a young boy, took the open-top South Gower bus and camped with friends here. In *Who Do You Wish Was With Us?* he wrote: 'Laughing on the cliff above the very long golden beach, we pointed out to each other, as though the other were blind, the great rock of the Worm's Head. The sea was out. We crossed over on slipping stones and stood, at last, triumphantly on the windy top. There was monstrous, thick grass there that made us spring-heeled and we laughed and bounced on it, scaring the sheep who ran up and down the battered sides like goats. Even on this calmest day a wind blew on the Worm.' He recalls his visit to the Outer Head: 'At the end of the humped and serpentine body, more gulls than I had ever seen before cried over their new dead and the droppings of ages.'

His own experiences here were a great inspiration for his work and he was cut off by the tide on more than one occasion on the Worm, as were the boys in *Who Do You Wish Was With Us?* He described his own experience: 'I stayed on that Worm from dusk to midnight, sitting on that top grass, frightened to go further in because of the rats and because of things I am ashamed to be frightened of. Then the tips of the reef began to poke out of the water and, perilously, I climbed along them to the shore.'

He considered moving here in 1953 but promptly dismissed the idea when his friend who owned the hotel explained that the nearest pub was in Port Eynon.

Low tide at Mewslade Bay and Thurba Head

141

Carry on along the coast to **Rhossili**, following the line of the cliffs where possible as this is more interesting than the large track. The cliffs below have been extensively quarried for limestone and you will cross the ramparts of an Iron Age fort. Pass the National Trust shop on the right and Worms Head Hotel on the left and continue along the road through the village to the bus stop. Bear left just after the bus stop on to a track around the church.

Turn left following the sign for the Coast Path and then turn right, heading for Rhossili Down, ignoring the turning on the left. Go through the gate onto National Trust land, and climb to the trig point on the The Beacon, the summit of **Rhossili Down**.

Look back for fantastic **views** of Worms Head. To the west is the south Pembrokeshire coastline and Caldey Island. If the visibility is really good, you can see Lundy Island just less than 50km away to the south and Hartland Point, the furthest western part of North Devon, some 64km away to the left of Lundy.

Rhossili Down, which rises to 193m, is an old beach level that was subsequently eroded by ice sheets during the penultimate Ice Age. The Bay has developed as the rocks that form its arms are harder Carboniferous limestone, whereas the softer Old Red Sandstone lying in the middle is less resistant to attack by Atlantic storms.

Outcrop of millstone grit on Rhossili Down with the remains of the radar station below

Walk 21 – Gower Coast NNR, Rhossili Down and Hardings Down

The platform underneath Rhossili Down is a solifluction terrace (see Walk 22). The lone house was once the Rectory for the churches at Rhossili and Llangennith and is now rented out by the National Trust (see Walk 18).

Drop down the hill from the trig point and, just after the path joins from the right, there is an obvious circle of stones marking the site of a **burial cairn** (see Walk 22). The boulders here comprise rounded quartz pebbles in sedimentary rocks formed during the Devonian period (see Geology). Looking to the east you can see the ridge of Cefn Bryn and stepped sea cliff of Pwlldu Head.

Take the right-hand fork when the path divides and, if you wish, descend the slope down to your right to visit the burial chambers of **Sweyne's Howes**. Climb back up to the ridge and drop down the front of the Down towards the campsite but turn right before the gate and take the path with the fence on your left. Turn left just after the house, cross over the stile into the field and pass through two fields with the fence on your left.

Cross the bridge over the stream, turn right and over the road leading to the house. Turn left after the swing gate, walk up past the paddocks and turn right, heading for Hardings Down ahead, and over the stile in the corner of the field. Keep the fence on your left and follow path to the road. Turn left and walk up the hill to the T-junction in **Llangennith** with St Cenydd's Church on your right and the Kings Head opposite.

Take the lane between the shop and the church and cross the stile in the hedge and follow the hedge on your right through to the next field. Cross the stile in the bottom right of the field, and pass through the trees and over the stile. Climb up the slope ahead to the top of the field and over the stile, ignoring the gate lower down on the left.

SWEYNE'S HOWES, RHOSSILI DOWN

Sweyne's Howes are two Neolithic chambered tombs delineated by an extensive cairn deposit and possible kerbing. The northern one is the better preserved with a chamber whose sides are formed by three large slabs of stone standing upright at right-angles to each other. The capstone, which has fallen off, lies on the ground between them. They date from 4000–2000 BC and the chambers would have been used for communal burials with grave goods for the dead to use in the afterlife.

Sweyne Forkbeard was the Viking king who is believed to have given his name to Swansea, and Howe is the Scandinavian name for a burial mound. However, these structures are not the burial chambers for Vikings as they predate them by over 2000 years.

Boulders of Devonian quartz conglomerate used to make the southern burial chamber of Sweyne's Howes

The path through the bramble briar brings you to an old farm lane where you turn right and then immediately left after the gate on a small path along the wall. Turn left on the well-used track and, where it straightens out, look for a path that cuts back up to the right where the slope has collapsed.

Climb into the centre of **Hardings Down** hill fort (see Walk 22) and ascend the impressive ditches and ramparts to meet a path where you carry straight on. This area has been used as grazing by commoners for centuries.

> Look over to the north to **Llanmadoc Hill** where there are the remains of another large Iron Age hill fort. Tankeylake Moor on its southern slope was the site of a battle between the clan on Hardings Down and the one occupying The Bulwark (see Walk 20).

Coming over the summit of Hardings Down, a great vista unfolds to the east of the heart of Gower with the ridge of Cefn Bryn running from left to right. The grassy track comes to a T-junction where you carry straight on to meet the well-used farm track below. Take the left-hand fork when the track divides and down to the white farmhouse at **East Cathan**. Turn left with the fence on your right and go over a stile into the field.

Follow this fence line through the fields, first with it on your left and then cross over a stile and follow it on your right, to Old Henllys. Cross over the stile on to the track that leads to the farm and then turn left before the gable end of the house. Cross

WALK 21 – GOWER COAST NNR, RHOSSILI DOWN AND HARDINGS DOWN

the field to a stile in the middle of the fence and through a small patch of woodland. Cross the field slightly to the left aiming for the stile on the right of the two large trees.

Head across the field aiming for a copse of trees and to a stile, ignoring the footpath that joins from the left. Follow the waymarked path to the derelict farm buildings at Newton, crossing over a footpath just before the stream. Take the farm track past the buildings and bear right at a fork and cross the stile. Head diagonally right across the large field to a stile in the corner. Ignore the farm track and cross diagonally to the right to a stile. Go straight ahead through the farm and back into **Pilton Green**.

View of the Old Rectory at the base of Rhossili Down with mist covering the ridge from The Beacon

WALK 22
Mewslade Bay, Fall Bay, Rhossili Down and Hardings Down

Start/finish	Pitton Farm car park (SS 4268 8765)
Distance	14.5km (8.9 miles)
Total ascent	365m
Time	4hr
Refreshments	Cafés, pub and shops in Rhossili; Kings Head pub in Llangennith

This is a great walk that combines the best of coastal Gower with upland Gower. You visit two of the finest beaches in Wales, with their spectacular limestone cliffs, and enjoy a fine view of Worms Head, a serpent of limestone snaking its way out to sea. This is followed by an ascent to the highest point on Gower and a traverse of Rhossili Down. The landscape oozes character when you imagine the people that carried out ritual ceremonies and burials here. A further ascent of Hardings Down to visit the large hill fort on its summit is followed by a pretty cross-country return to the start.

Turn left out of the car park in **Pitton**, down the road and turn right at the bend and take the path down the valley to where a path leaves on the right in front of a limestone outcrop with a cave.

There is an alternative route which is possible if the tide is low enough with a continuous stretch of sand from Mewslade Bay to Fall Bay. If you wish to take this option, continue down the valley and scramble down to Mewslade Bay. Cross in front of the cliffs looking for an impressive sea cave and then on to the far end of Fall Bay. Scramble up the rocks and climb the slope to rejoin the main route at Tears Point.

Otherwise, turn right on to the Coast Path, climbing out of the valley to meet a path where you turn left and then left again shortly afterwards. This runs along the cliff above **Mewslade Bay** which has a beautiful sandy beach at low tide. The path rejoins the Coast Path and follows a limestone drystone wall which borders the medieval field system of The Viel (see Walk 21).

Continue around the head of **Fall Bay**, dropping down the slade to the beach if the tide is out and if you wish to explore this interesting area, rejoining the route

WALK 22 – MEWSLADE BAY, FALL BAY, ROSSILI DOWN AND HARDINGS DOWN

at Tears Point. The two tiers of steep cliff on the left are popular with rock climbers and offer some spectacular routes.

The path comes to **Tears Point** where the Coast Path swings right to the Lookout Station which was once a Victorian coastguard base and is now staffed by Coastwatch. There is a fine view of the causeway and Worms Head from here (see Walk 19).

Carry along the coast to **Rhossili**, following the line of the cliffs where possible as this is more interesting than the large track. The cliffs below have been extensively quarried for limestone and you will cross the ramparts of an Iron Age fort. Pass the National Trust shop on the right and Worms Head Hotel on the left and continue along the road through the village to the bus stop. Bear left just after the bus stop on to a track around the church.

Turn left following the sign for the Coast Path and then turn right, heading for Rhossili Down, ignoring the turning on the left. Go through the gate onto National Trust land and climb to The Beacon, marked by a trig point.

The **platform** underneath Rhossili Down is a solifluction terrace. The lone house was once the Rectory for the churches at Rhossili and Llangennith and is now rented out by the National Trust (see Walk 18).

Look back for fantastic **views** of Worms Head. To the west is the south Pembrokeshire coastline and Caldey Island. If the visibility is really good, you can see Lundy Island just less than 50km away to the south and Hartland Point, the furthest western part of North Devon, some 64km away to the left of Lundy.

Walking along the lower coast path above Mewslade Bay

Admiring the view of Worms Head from Rhossili Down

SOLIFLUCTION TERRACE

The path leading north along Rhossili Down from The Beacon

The narrow strip of land at the base of Rhossili Down is a solifluction terrace formed at the end of the last glaciation by large quantities of material sliding down the scarp face of the Down, forming an apron at its base. The sea is constantly eroding this, forming a cliff of loose material.

Rhossili Down, which rises to 193m, is an old beach level that was subsequently eroded by ice sheets during the penultimate Ice Age. The Bay has developed as the rocks that form its arms are harder Carboniferous limestone, whereas the softer Old Red Sandstone lying in the middle is less resistant to attack by Atlantic storms.

Drop down the hill from the trig point and, just after the path joins from the right, there is an obvious circle of stones marking the site of a **burial cairn**. The boulders here comprise rounded quartz pebbles in sedimentary rock that was formed during the Devonian period (see Geology). Looking to the east is the ridge of Cefn Bryn and stepped sea cliff of Pwlldu Head.

CAIRN CIRCLE, RHOSSILI DOWN

Cairn circle on Rhossili Down

A circle of upright stones surrounds a level platform around 0.3m high, which is an unusual variant on the standard ring cairn. Many of the stones protrude above the level of the platform indicating that they may have originally supported an earth- or stone-filled rim. In the centre is a small hollow which may be all that remains of a burial cist.

Take the right-hand fork when the path divides and, if you wish, descend the slope down to your right to visit the burial chambers of **Sweyne's Howes** (see Walk 21). Climb back up to the ridge and drop down the front of the Down

WALK 22 – MEWSLADE BAY, FALL BAY, RHOSSILI DOWN AND HARDINGS DOWN

towards the campsite but turn right before the gate and take the path with the fence on your left. Turn left just after the house, cross over the stile into the field and pass through two fields with the fence on your left.

Cross the bridge over the stream, turn right and over the road leading to the house. Turn left after the swing gate, walk up past the paddocks and turn right, heading for Hardings Down ahead, and go over the stile in the corner of the field. Keep the fence on your left and follow the path to the road. Turn left and walk up the hill to the T-junction in **Llangennith** with St Cenydd's Church on your right and the Kings Head opposite.

Take the lane between the shop and the church, cross the stile in the hedge and follow the hedge on your right through the next field. Cross the stile in the bottom right of the field, and pass through the trees and over the stile. Climb up the slope ahead to the top of the field and over the stile, ignoring the gate lower down on the left.

The path through the bramble briar brings you to an old farm lane where you turn right and then immediately left after the gate on a small path along the wall. Turn left on the well-used track and, where it straightens out, look for a path that cuts back up to the right after the second area where the slope has collapsed.

Climb into the centre of **Hardings Down** hill fort and ascend the impressive ditches and ramparts to meet a path where you turn right. This area has been used as grazing by commoners for centuries.

Continue in the same direction, following the path down the hill to meet a path where you turn right and descend across the slope to meet a track. Cross over the first track and bear right on the lower one heading for the derelict stone buildings at West Cathan. Leave the track by turning left on the footpath that passes in between the stone buildings. Follow the path over the fields to the derelict farm building at **Kingshall**. Cross over the stream, turn right and then left through the patch of woodland and over a stile into the field.

Keep the ditch on your left for two fields and then cross over a stile, turn right and follow the hedge to meet a bridleway. Turn right and immediately left on to a path which you take to Pitton, ignoring any turnings on the right or left. Turn right at the main road in **Pitton** and first left back to the start.

HARDINGS DOWN HILL FORT

This hill has the remains of three Iron Age hill forts dating from around 2000 years ago. Evidence has been found for a number of house platforms within the enclosure and excavations have revealed a cobbled entrance and pottery dating to 100–50BC. The two smaller forts would have housed only a few families and it is a mystery as to why they are outside the main fort.

WALK 23
Llanmadoc Hill, Llangennith, Burry Holms and Broughton Bay

Start/finish	Car park, Llanmadoc (SS 4398 9349)
Distance	13.5km (8.1 miles)
Total ascent	270m
Time	3hr 30min
Refreshments	Kings Head pub in Llangennith; Lagadranta Café

The route climbs to Llanmadoc Hill, one of the highest points in Gower and a fine site for The Bulwark, the most impressive of the Iron Age hill forts on the peninsula. From here, a superb 360-degree vista unfolds of the whole of Gower. The route then descends to Llangennith and then along the beach to Burry Holms and around the sand dunes to Broughton Bay. Hill's Tor has one of the finest landscape views in Wales of Whiteford Burrows National Nature Reserve and the route also visits Landimore Marsh, a rich environment for birds.

Broughton Beach and Llanmadoc Hill from Foxhole Point

Walk 23 – Llanmadoc Hill, Llangennith, Burry Holms and Broughton Bay

Turn left out of the car park in **Llanmadoc** and walk up the lane with St Madoc's Church on your right.

> The impressive Swiss-style house is the **Rectory** and its design was inspired by the Reverend JD Davies' holiday in Switzerland. He was the Rector from 1860 to 1911 and a skilled carpenter, both building this unusual house and carving the oak altar in the church.

Just afterwards, keep left to the triangular green where you bear right and follow the sign for the bridleway on the right and carry on straight ahead, ignoring the path on the right.

This old sunken track leads to the open hillside where you take the path that heads diagonally up the slope to the left. Cross over a path and continue straight ahead with the path climbing to the left. This meets the right of way coming up from the left where you take the path on the right that leads up the gulley on the right ahead. Cross over the next path and continue up the gulley, which is actually the western-most defence of the fort, to the ridge. All of these ditches are part of an extensive Iron Age hill fort called The Bulwark (see Walk 24).

> Some of the **finest views in Gower** are from here. To the north-east is the extensive salt marsh and tidal flats of the Loughor Estuary, the South Wales coalfield and the Brecon Beacons beyond. To the west is the south Pembrokeshire coast including Caldey Island and the furthest point of St Govan's Head at 46km. The Devon coastline can be seen to the south on a clear day.

Once you have explored **The Bulwark**, head west along the ridge to the large pile of stones, which is just one of a number of Iron Age burial cairns on the hill. The path then drops down slightly off the ridge to a crossroads where you take the path that climbs up to the right to the trig point, ignoring the wider path that descends to the left. Turn left at the trig point marking the summit of **Llanmadoc Hill** and descend to meet a path where you turn right. Down to your left is Tankeylake Moor, reputed to have been the site of a bloody battle between two local clans (see Walk 20).

Follow this until you can take a small path that drops down to the left in line with a building. Cross over the stile to the left of the house, over the track and stile to cross the field to another stile.

Turn right at the road down to the King's Head in **Llangennith**. Turn left down the lane on the right of St Cenydd's Church and take the next footpath on the right. Follow the fence on your right to a stile and cross over. Keep the fence on your left and cross the stile, following the footpath to College Mill. Cross over the driveway to the house and turn right along the stream to the road.

Turn right and then left at the bend on to the footpath. Turn right at a T-junction and follow the path across Llangennith Moors to a track where you turn left to the beach. It is possible that treasure from the wreck of the Dollar Ship still remains buried in the sand in the beach in front of you (see Walk 20).

> The **strandline** has an interesting collection of seashells, giving a clue to the species that live in this high-energy sandy beach which faces due west and bears the brunt of huge Atlantic rollers during storms. These include oyster, razor shell, prickly cockle, sand gaper and carpet shells, although the oysters may be remnants from the large oyster fishery based in Port Eynon in the past.

Turn right along the beach to Spaniard Rocks and **Burry Holms**. It is possible to explore the island when the tide is out where you can see the remains of an Iron Age fort.

WALK 23 – LLANMADOC HILL, LLANGENNITH, BURRY HOLMS AND BROUGHTON BAY

BURRY HOLMS

Burry Holms

Around 9000 years ago Burry Holms was an inland hill, surrounded by a wide coastal plain covered with a pine and birch woodland almost 20km from the sea. Charcoal found on the site suggests that Mesolithic people were managing the woodland as a renewable resource. They did this by burning small patches to create clearings in which new and nutritious plants grew. This attracted deer which they captured, moving on once large trees established themselves once more. Small tools used for hunting and fishing and made of flint, wood and bone have been discovered here.

The island was occupied later during the Iron Age. The remains of an early Christian hermitage have been found on the inner east end of the headland and the remnants of the succeeding 12th century church and ancillary buildings can be seen today.

Head north-east from Spaniard Rocks on the Coast Path through the dunes to Bluepool Corner.

It is worth dropping down on the east side of the bay to see the large circular natural **rock pool** 5m in diameter and almost as deep. On the opposite side of the bay is a sea arch called the Three Chimneys.

In 1800 a fisherman called John Richard found a quantity of gold *moidores*, **Portuguese gold coins**, and doubloons among the rocks here. Others have found coins, including divers searching the seabed.

Just around the corner to the south-west of a sea arch called the Three Chimneys is **Culver Hole** in which the remains of 41 bodies have been excavated, dating to the Middle Bronze Age, 1450–1000 BC. Other finds included Early Iron Age pottery, a late Celtic female figurine, coins and brooches from the second century AD and a ninth-century brooch.

The Coast Path leads to **Twlc Point** and around the back of Broughton Bay. If the tide is low enough, it is possible to walk along the beach around Prissen's Tor and Hills Tor and rejoin the route at Cwm Ivy Tor. This allows Prissen's Tor Cave, also known as Spritsail Tor Cave, a bone cave to be explored in the headland. Otherwise, follow the path through the back of the dunes at Delvid Burrows to a gate and then straight on to where the track turns right. Refreshments are available at the Lagadranta Café. According to Gower legend Lagadranta farm is the last place in Gower where the Verry Volk were seen.

Carry on along the Welsh Coast Path through the dunes and then up the slope to **Hills Tor**. The view from **Hills Tor**, overlooking Whiteford NNR, is one of the finest in Gower.

It is possible to descend to the beach between Prissen's Tor and Hills Tor and investigate the **bone cave** in the headland. Prissen's Tor Cave is also known as Spritsail Tor Cave.

Follow the Coast Path along the top of the cliff and then descend down some steps through ash woodland of The Conygaer to arrive below **Cwm Ivy Tor**, a large limestone outcrop. Stay on the track, ignoring the turning on the left. Follow the track underneath the limestone outcrop and climb back up the road to the start in **Llanmadoc**.

Bone cave at Prissen's or Spritsail Tor at Broughton Bay

WALK 24

Llanmadoc Hill, Broughton Bay and Whiteford NNR

Start/finish	Car park, Llanmadoc (SS 4398 9349)
Distance	16km (10 miles)
Total ascent	235m
Time	4hr 30min
Refreshments	Lagadranta Café and Cwm Ivy Café

The ascent at the beginning of this walk takes you to the summit of Llanmadoc Hill, one of the highest points in Gower and a fine site for The Bulwark, the most impressive of the Iron Age hill forts on the peninsula. From here, a superb 360-degree vista unfolds of the whole of Gower. The route descends to Broughton Bay and then to Hills Tor from where you have one of the finest landscape views in Wales of Whiteford Burrows National Nature Reserve. A circuit of this passes the marsh at Burry Pill and Cwm Ivy Marsh, a rich environment for birds.

Turn left out of the car park in **Llanmadoc** and up the lane with St Madoc's Church on the right.

> The impressive Swiss-style house is the **Rectory** and its design was inspired by the reverend JD Davies' holiday in Switzerland. He was the rector from 1860 to 1911 and a skilled carpenter, both building this unusual house and carving the oak altar in the church.

Just afterwards, bear left to the triangular green and follow the sign for the bridleway on the right and carry on straight ahead, ignoring the path on the right.
This old sunken track leads to the open hillside where you take the path that heads diagonally up the slope to the left. Cross over a path and continue straight ahead with the path climbing to the left. This meets the right of way coming up from the left where you take the path on the right that leads up the gulley on the right ahead. Cross over the next path and continue up the gulley, which is actually the western-most defence of a fort, to the ridge. All of these ditches are part of the extensive Iron Age hill fort called The Bulwark.

WALKING ON GOWER

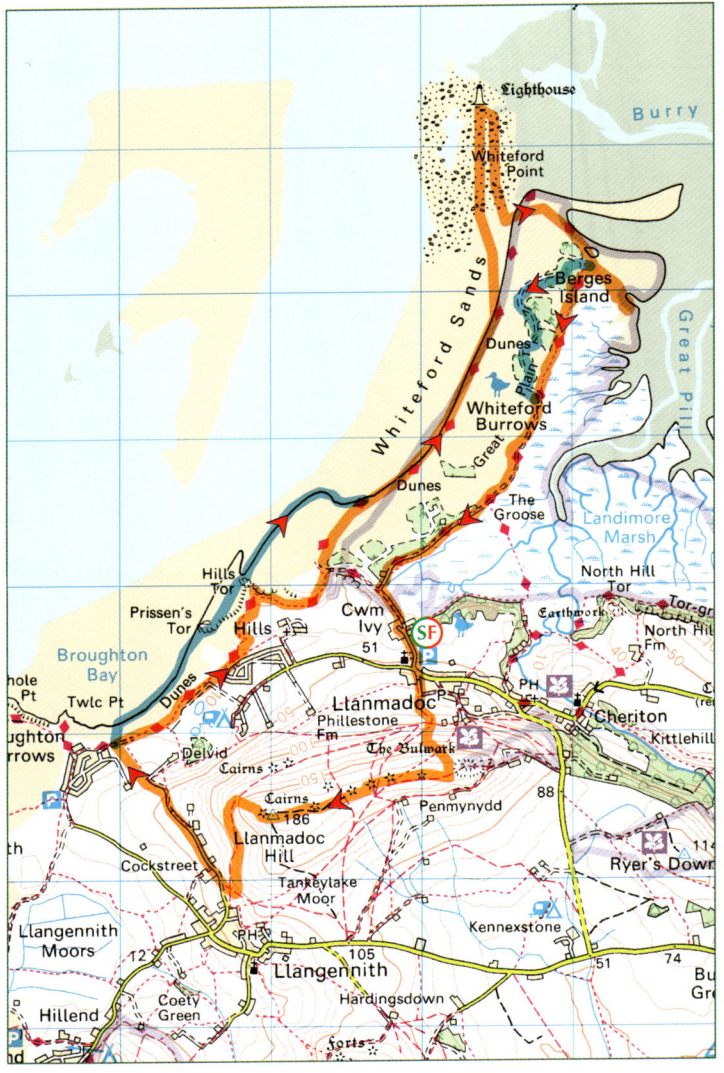

WALK 24 – LLANMADOC HILL, BROUGHTON BAY AND WHITEFORD NNR

Some of the **finest views in Gower** are from here. To the north-east is the extensive salt marsh and tidal flats of the Loughor Estuary, the South Wales coalfield and the Brecon Beacons beyond. To the west is the south Pembrokeshire coast including Caldey Island and furthest point is St Govan's Head at 46km. The Devon coastline can be seen to the south on a clear day.

THE BULWARK (700–100BC)

Llanmadoc Hill is one of highest points on Gower at 186m and is made of Old Red Sandstone. The numerous ditches and embankments at its eastern end are the remains of a large Iron Age hill fort, The Bulwark. The widely-spaced ramparts suggest a primarily pastoral function but defence must have been an important consideration or the fort would not have been situated in such a strategic position on the edge of the Hill. The Hill is also covered with 14 Bronze Age cairns.

From here there are great views of Rhossili Bay and the magnificent Worms Head. Once you have explored The Bulwark, head west along the ridge to the large pile of stones, which is just one of a number of Iron Age burial cairns on the hill. The path then drops down slightly off the ridge to a crossroads where you take the path that climbs up to the right to the trig point marking the summit of **Llanmadoc Hill**, ignoring the wider path that descends to the left. Continue west along the ridge from the trig point and descend the hill with a stony cairn on your right.

Look out for boulders of quartz conglomerate, containing rounded pebbles, as you descend the ridge. The path divides just after these boulders. Take the one that goes straight on, to meet a path that runs across the hill in front of another

Prissen's or Spritsail Tor with the bone cave at Broughton Bay

The track through the centre of the NNR from Whiteford Point

outcrop of conglomerate; turn left here in the direction of Worms Head. This drops diagonally down the slope to meet another where you turn right to reach the road.

Turn right along the tarmac road and when it ends follow the path signposted Broughton Beach. Leave this track at a bend, again following the sign for the beach. Cross over a couple of fields, keeping the fence just on your right, and turn right on the Wales Coast Path, signposted Llanmadoc. Shortly afterwards, if the tide is low enough, you can take a small path to the top of the dunes and drop down to the beach and rejoin the main route where it meets the beach near Cwm Ivy Tor.

Otherwise, follow the path through the back of the dunes at Delvid Burrows to a gate and then straight on to where the track turns right. Refreshments are available at the Lagadranta Café. A Gower legend has it that Lagadranta farm is the last place in Gower where the Verry Volk were seen. Carry on along the Coast Path through the dunes and then up the slope to **Hills Tor**. The view from Hills Tor, overlooking Whiteford NNR, is one of the finest in Gower.

It is possible to descend to the beach between Prissen's Tor and Hills Tor and investigate the **bone cave** in the headland. Prissen's Tor Cave is also known as Spritsail Tor Cave.

Follow the coast path along the top of the cliff which then descends down some steps through ash woodland to **Cwm Ivy Tor**, a large limestone outcrop,

WALK 24 – LLANMADOC HILL, BROUGHTON BAY AND WHITEFORD NNR

where there is a gate to a track and an interpretation board. Turn left through the gate, signposted Whiteford and follow the sandy track through the dunes to a fenced off area. This is to protect ground-nesting birds such as lapwing, during the breeding season.

Turn right and walk along the track to the top of the beach and follow this through **Whiteford NNR** (see Walk 25) all the way to **Whiteford Point**.

Whiteford Lighthouse

The **strandline** at the top of the beach is a fascinating place to explore as it gives many clues as to what is living in the intertidal area. Look out for different shells such as mussels, razorfish, clams and whelks. The sand spit is constantly changing position and shape in response to wave action and tidal currents.

The area around **Whiteford Lighthouse** (see Walk 25), accessible at low tide, has an extensive mussel bed, and quicksand that still contains unexploded bombs from World War 2.

Once around Whiteford Point, walk along the top of the beach and then leave the strand line by heading for the left of the conifers with a drainage channel now on your left. Continue past the second group of conifer to a bird hide. The best time to visit this is very close to a full neap tide. At high water you can see pintail, great northern diver, small flocks of merganser and larger flocks of eider. As it starts to ebb, look for Slavonian grebe, with brent geese and various waders likely congregating on the shore. From the bird hide, return along the southern shore of the spit to the edge of the woodland.

You have the option of either following the path along the edge of the saltmarsh through the trees or taking the path that crosses through the centre of the dunes. They merge later on, where you continue with the marsh on your left, passing Burrows Cottage and another bird hide (which is at its best on a big high tide when Cwm Ivy Marsh is flooded by the tide passing through a breach in **The Groose** sea wall). The track comes to a T-junction where you turn left and back to the start. This is a good area for seeing various bird species, including flocks of lapwing in winter, and grey herons feeding in the channels.

WALK 25
Whiteford National Nature Reserve

Start/finish	Car park, Llanmadoc (SS 4398 9349)
Distance	10.5km (6.4 miles)
Total ascent	50m
Time	2hr 30min
Refreshments	Cwm Ivy Café

This relaxing and easy walk is based on the sand dune part of Whiteford NNR, taking in the great expanse of Whiteford Sands and the tranquil salt marsh. Whiteford Lighthouse can be visited if you time the walk to arrive at Whiteford Point on a low spring tide. Winter is a good time to visit to see overwintering waders and wildfowl, while spring and summer are the times to come to experience the multitude of different orchids that can be found in the special dune habitat.

Turn right out of the car park in **Llanmadoc** and go down the hill to the end of the road. Continue following the footpath signs for the beach. The spit of land in front is Whiteford NNR. Ignore the first turning on the right and carry on along the track to where it bends to the left under **Cwm Ivy Tor**.

Turn right through the gate, and follow the sandy track through the dunes to a fenced off area. This is to protect ground-nesting birds such as lapwing during the breeding season.

Turn right and walk along the track to the top of the beach and follow this all the way to **Whiteford Point**.

The **strandline** at the top of the beach is a fascinating place to explore as it gives many clues as to what is living in the intertidal area. Look out for different shells such as mussels, razor-fish, clams and whelks. Unfortunately, this is also the place where all the plastic litter congregates. The sand spit is constantly changing position and shape in response to wave action and tidal currents.

Once around Whiteford Point, walk along the top of the beach and then leave the strand line by heading for the left of the conifers with a drainage channel now on your left. Continue past the second group of conifer to a bird hide. The best

The conifer plantation and bird hide to the east of Whiteford Point

WHITEFORD NATIONAL NATURE RESERVE

The area of Whiteford Burrows is thought to have developed from a glacial moraine that was later covered in sand dunes. This is a special habitat because of the wet areas between the sand dunes called dune slacks. The sand is rich in calcium due to the abundant shell fragments blown in from the beach. At least 250 species of flowering plants have been recorded, making it one of the richest dune-slack systems in the UK, with up to 10 different orchid species flowering at the same time.

The abundance of wild flowers provides an excellent habitat for a wide variety of butterflies and other insects. Look out for the common blue, small blue, dark green fritillary and grayling. The salt marsh and mudflats are also rich in wildlife and particularly important for wintering wildfowl and wading birds. Look out for oystercatcher, curlew, lapwing, redshank and snipe.

time to visit this is very close to a full neap tide. At high water you can see pintail, great northern diver, small flocks of merganser and larger flocks of eider, and as it

WHITEFORD LIGHTHOUSE

The approach to Whiteford Lighthouse from Whiteford Point on a low spring tide

Whiteford Lighthouse is the only surviving intertidal cast-iron lighthouse in the UK and is accessible only at low water. This ornate Victorian structure, built in 1865 by the Llanelli Harbour and Burry Navigation Commissioners to mark the shoals of Whiteford Point, is almost 14m tall. The heavy cast-iron plates that make up the seven bands are bolted together with external flanges, unlike other cast-iron towers where they are internal. The glazing bars are copper, a reminder that Llanelli was once an important copper-exporting port.

A large roost of cormorants uses the lighthouse, and as many as 158 birds have been recorded; they breed on St Margaret's Island near Tenby.

The area around the Lighthouse has an extensive mussel bed, and quicksand that still contains unexploded bombs from World War 2.

WALK 25 – WHITEFORD NATIONAL NATURE RESERVE

starts to ebb Slavonian grebe is frequently seen here, with brent geese and various waders congregating on the shore. From the bird hide, return along the southern shore of the spit to the edge of the woodland.

You have the option of following the path along the edge of the saltmarsh through the trees or taking the path that crosses through the centre of the dunes. These paths merge later, where you continue with the marsh on your left, passing Burrows Cottage and another bird hide (which is at its best on a big high tide when Cwm Ivy Marsh is flooded by the tide passing through a breach in **The Groose** sea wall). The track comes to a T-junction where you turn left and back to the start.

Walking on Gower

WALK 26

Landimore Marsh, Cheriton, Burry Pill and Weobley Castle

Start/finish	Car park at the end of the road, Landimore (SS 4645 9353)
Distance	9km (5.5 miles)
Total ascent	80m
Time	2hr
Refreshments	Britannia Inn in Llanmadoc
Note	The car park and track along the marsh may be inundated during high water on the largest spring tides of the year. Be sure to check tide times and heights.

An early start will be rewarded with a hauntingly beautiful atmosphere as you walk west along the edge of the salt marsh from the pretty village of Landimore round to Cheriton. This passes through the wetland section of Whiteford National Nature Reserve and wildlife interest is diverse and abundant. Grey heron, little egret and raptors of various kinds will inevitably be encountered. The inland part of the walk follows the picturesque valley of Burry Pill before crossing back to the coast to Weobley Castle via the standing stone of Samson Jack.

Start at the car parking area at the end of the road in **Landimore**. With the salt marsh in front of you, turn left onto the National Trust land of Cors Landimore Marsh, which is part of Whiteford NNR (see Walk 25).

> This area was used as a firing range during World War 2 but is now grazed by **ponies and sheep**; the latter are herded off the marsh during high spring tides, whereas the ponies are content and safe to stand calmly in the rising water.

Follow the track along the Coast Path, bordered on your left by ash woodland growing on **Tor Gro**, a steep north-facing Carboniferous limestone scarp. There are the remains of many limekilns adjacent to the track at Landimore.

Walk 26 – Landimore Marsh, Cheriton, Burry Pill and Weobley Castle

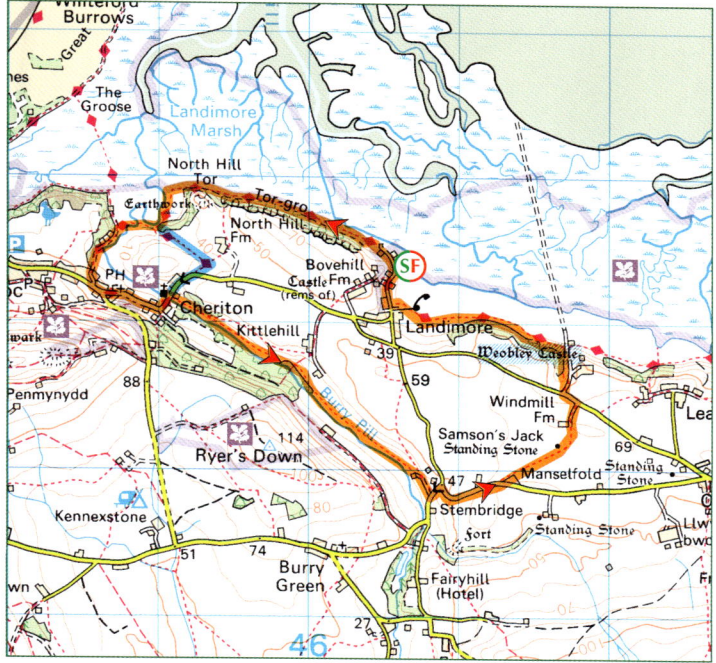

The **limestone scarp** has been significantly altered by extensive quarrying in the 1900s when the limestone was transported by boat along the creeks in the salt marsh, some of which were canalised to aid navigation.

The track turns inland when it meets the Burry Pill; the path crosses a footbridge with the impressive limestone hill of **North Hill Tor** on your left.

Not surprisingly, this prominent feature is the location for an earthwork, the remains of **Nottle Tor Camp**. It is thought likely that this was a timber medieval castle owned by the Turbervilles in the 12th century.

Continue on the path with the Pill on your right. You can see across the salt marsh behind the white cottages to Berry Hill woodland, with the sand dune area of the NNR further to the right.

Snowdrops at St Cadoc's Church, Cheriton

If the walk coincides with a high spring tide and the Pill is not crossable, follow the diversion along the footpath on the left that will bring you to the church. Otherwise, follow the Coast Path signs over the Pill and turn left on the other side to the village. Turn left and left again onto the road, passing the Britannia Inn and down the road to the church in **Cheriton** in the bottom of the valley. Turn right opposite the church, signposted Stembridge, and cross over the stile into the ash woodland with **Burry Pill** running down to your right. At the end of the patch of woodland, take the path to the right, ignoring the one up to the left.

This brings you to a crossroads where you carry straight on towards Stembridge.

Follow the marked footpath through the fields to a house and follow the footpath signs to the road, ignoring the footpath that ascends the hill up to the left.

Turn left at the road in **Stembridge**, climb the hill and take the next footpath on the left. After the farm buildings, keep the fence on your left to **Samson's Jack**, a large standing stone. Cross into the next field and follow the fence on the left to **Windmill Farm**. Follow the tarmac road left down the hill with a fine view of Weobley Castle ahead. Turn right and then left, signposted to the Castle, and then left a few metres afterwards and along the fence on the right side of the valley, past **Weobley Castle** (see Walk 29).

Turn left on to the Coast Path at the bottom of the field, signposted Landimore. Follow the path through the fields, with Hambury Wood Wildlife Trust Nature Reserve on your left.

Leave the cliff as it swings around to the left near Landimore, crossing the fields to the road, following the Coast Path signs. Up above you on the cliff top are the remains of Bovehill Castle, a fortified manor house. Turn right, passing the National Trust's Bove Hill on the left and an old limekiln, and return to the start in **Landimore**.

WALK 27

Landimore Marsh, Arthur's Stone, Llanrhidian and Weobley Castle

Start/finish	Car park at end of road, Landimore (SS 4645 9353)
Distance	16km (10 miles)
Total ascent	160m
Time	4hr 30min
Refreshments	Britannia Inn in Llanmadoc; pubs and garage in Llanrhidian
Note	The car park and track along the marsh may be inundated during high water on the largest spring tides of the year. Be sure to check tide times and heights.

An early start will be rewarded with a hauntingly beautiful atmosphere as you walk west along the edge of the salt marsh from the pretty village of Landimore to Cheriton. This passes through the wetland section of Whiteford National Nature Reserve and wildlife interest is diverse and abundant. Grey heron, little egret and raptors of various kinds will inevitably be encountered. The inland part of the walk follows the picturesque valley of Burry Pill before climbing up to Cefn Bryn and Arthur's Stone. The return is via Llanrhidian and along the marsh via Weobley Castle.

Start at the car parking area at the end of the road in **Landimore**. With the salt marsh in front of you, turn left onto the National Trust land of Cors Landimore Marsh which is part of Whiteford NNR (see Walk 25).

> This area was used as a firing range during World War 2 but is now grazed by **ponies and sheep**; the latter are herded off the marsh during high spring tides, whereas the ponies are content and safe to stand calmly in the rising water.

Follow the track along the Coast Path, bordered on your left by ash woodland growing on **Tor Gro**, a steep north facing Carboniferous limestone scarp. There are the remains of many limekilns adjacent to the track at Landimore.

> The **limestone scarp** has been significantly altered by extensive quarrying in the 1900s when the limestone was transported by boat along the creeks in the salt marsh, some of which were canalised to aid navigation.

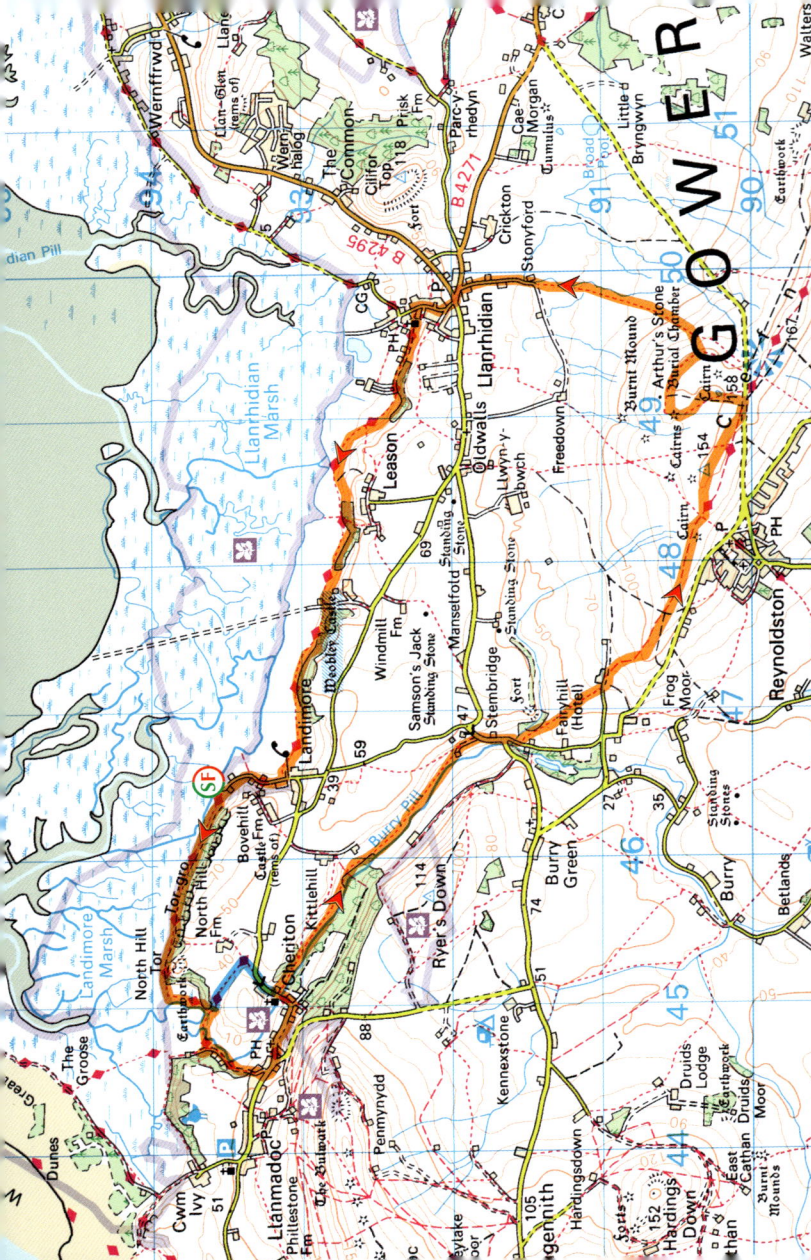

WALK 27 – LANDIMORE MARSH, ARTHUR'S STONE, LLANRHIDIAN AND WEOBLEY CASTLE

The upper tidal reaches of Burry Pill

The track turns inland when it meets Burry Pill and then the path crosses a footbridge with the impressive limestone hill of **North Hill Tor** on your left.

Not surprisingly, this prominent feature is the location for an earthwork, the remains of **Nottle Tor Camp**. It is thought likely that this was a timber medieval castle owned by the Turbervilles in the 12th century.

Continue on the path with the Pill on your right.
If your walk coincides with a high spring tide and the Pill is not crossable, follow the diversion on the footpath on the left that will bring you to the church. Otherwise, follow the Coast Path signs over the Pill and turn left on the other side to the village. Turn left and left again onto the road, passing the Britannia Inn and down the road to the church in **Cheriton** in the bottom of the valley. Turn right opposite the church, signposted Stembridge, and cross over the stile into the ash woodland with **Burry Pill** running down to your right. At the end of the patch of woodland, take the path to the right, ignoring the one up to the left.

This brings you to a crossroads where you carry straight on towards Stembridge. It is worth exploring the very old bridge over the stream on your right.

Follow the marked footpath through the fields to a house and follow the footpath signs to the road in **Stembridge**, ignoring the footpath that ascends the hill up to the left.

Follow the road to the bottom of the valley where you turn left, marked Fairy Hill Restaurant, and then left onto a footpath that crosses the field diagonally up to the left. Notice the mature woodland on the steep slope in the valley on your left. This was the site of an Iron Age promontory fort.

Follow the hedge to another stile and to the tarmac road at Hillend where you turn left and then right through a gate. Turn left soon where you join a track and take the one that climbs the hillside, ignoring the one on the left. Stay on this bridleway, heading for the trig point on Cefn Bryn (see Walk 8). There is a fantastic view north of the Loughor Estuary, west to Llanmadoc Hill and north-east to the South Wales coalfield and the Brecon Beacons beyond.

Swing left when you approach the car parking area and head north along the path, with a pool on your right, and then left to the pile of stones, Great Carn. Cross over to the large boulders of **Arthur's Stone** (see Walk 28). There are around 60 piles of stones on Cefn Bryn. Some of these are Bronze Age while others were made by farmers clearing the fields.

Facing north, take the path on the right, ignoring the smaller path straight ahead. As you walk, Broad Pool (see Walk 8) can be seen ahead over to your left

17th century Grade II listed three-arch packhorse bridge across Burry Pill

WALK 27 – LANDIMORE MARSH, ARTHUR'S STONE, LLANRHIDIAN AND WEOBLEY CASTLE

The route along the edge of Landimore Marsh, part of Whiteford National Nature Reserve

and further left again you can make out the sculpted ramparts of an Iron Age hill fort on the summit on Cilifor Top.

Turn left off this track down a path that descends the slope in line with Broad Pool. At the bottom of the slope follow an indistinct track across the moor heading in the direction of Cilifor hill fort and a white farmhouse. Halfway across the moor, head for the farm building at **Stonyford** on your left and then drop into a small gulley with an area of gorse beyond. From here, you will be able to see a stile in the fence in line with the gable end of the farmhouse.

Bear right once you have crossed the fence and follow the lane with the farmhouse on your right. This brings you to the main road at the garage where you turn left and then right down the hill to the church in **Llanrhidian**. You have a choice of two pubs in the village, the Welcome to Town and the Dolphin.

You can clearly see the ramparts of the hill fort on Cilifor Top at the end of the lane near the garage in line with the B4295.

Turn left between the two standing stones into the churchyard and, with the church on your right, take the path to the left that crosses the wall over a stone step. The path then reaches the road where you turn left, joining the Coast Path. The woodland on the left is Llanrhidian Hill Nature Reserve, owned and managed by the Wildlife Trust for South and West Wales.

The road ends and becomes a path that crosses the top of a field, and at a junction of paths, take the route indicated by the blue marker which runs along

Weobley Castle

the top of the field with the salt marsh on your right. This comes to a gate, from where there is a view of Weobley Castle ahead. Ignore the permissive footpath that climbs up through Leason Wood and carry straight on in the direction of the castle.

The path starts to climb up the hill on a very old stony lane, then take a footpath on the right towards Landimore. This enters a large field which you leave half-way along via a stile in the fence with a blue Coast Path arrow, and continue to a track which you cross over. Just beyond is a small valley and, if you wish to explore **Weobley Castle**, take the footpath on the left which leads up the left edge of the grassy field in the valley to join the track and turn left to the entrance (see Walk 29). The Castle is well worth exploring and offers a superb view of the Loughor Estuary.

Otherwise, follow the path through the fields with the woodland on your left; this is Hambury Wood Wildlife Trust Nature Reserve. Turn left on to the Coast Path at the bottom of the field, signposted Landimore. Follow the path through the fields, with Hambury Wood Wildlife Trust Nature Reserve on your left.

Leave the cliff as it swings around to the left near Landimore, crossing the fields to the road, following the Coast Path signs. Up above you on the cliff top are the remains of Bovehill Castle, a fortified manor house.

Turn right, passing the National Trust's Bove Hill on the left and an old lime-kiln, and return to the start in **Landimore**.

WALK 28

Cefn Bryn, Llanrhidian and Weobley Castle

Start/finish	Cefn Bryn (SS 4907 9004)
Distance	10.5km (6.4 miles)
Total ascent	200m
Time	3hr
Refreshments	Pubs and garage at Llanrhidian

This walk starts on the second highest point in Gower giving excellent panoramic views of the peninsula and beyond. The dramatic Arthur's Stone is encountered near the start and the route then drops down to Llanrhidian where you have the choice of two pubs for refreshment. The walk continues along the edge of woodland just above the vast salt marsh of the Loughor Estuary to the impressive Weobley Castle, before traversing across farmland to climb to the ridge of Cefn Bryn once again.

From the car parking area on the summit of **Cefn Bryn** (see Walk 8), head north along the path, with a pool on your right, to **Arthur's Stone**, on the left of which is Great Carn. There are numerous cairns marked on the map in this area. There is a fantastic view north to the Loughor Estuary, to the west to Llanmadoc Hill and to the north-east to the South Wales coalfield and the Brecon Beacons beyond.

Facing north, take the path on the right, ignoring the smaller path straight ahead. As you walk, Broad Pool (see Walk 8) can be seen ahead over to your left and further left again you can make out the sculpted ramparts of an Iron Age hill fort on the summit on Cilifor Top.

Turn left off this track down a path which descends the slope in line with Broad Pool. At the bottom of the slope follow an indistinct track across the moor heading in the direction of Cilifor hill fort and a white farmhouse. Halfway across the moor, head for the farm building at **Stonyford** on your left and then drop into a small gulley with an area of gorse beyond. From here, you will be able to see a stile in the fence in line with the gable end of the farmhouse.

Bear right once you have crossed the fence and follow the lane with the farmhouse on your right. This brings you to the main road at the garage where you turn left and then right down the hill to the church in **Llanrhidian**. You have a choice of two pubs in the village, the Welcome to Town and the Dolphin.

WALKING ON GOWER

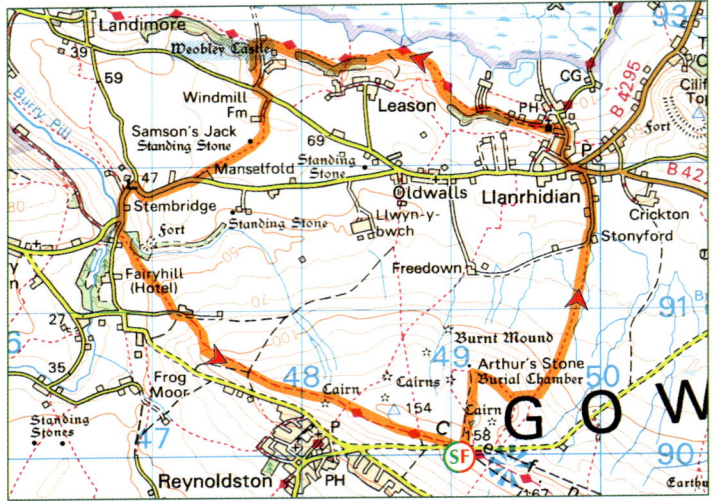

You can clearly see the ramparts of the hill fort on Cilifor Top at the end of the lane near the garage in line with the B4295.

Turn left between the two standing stones into the churchyard and, with the church on your right, take the path to the left that crosses the wall over a stone step. The path then reaches the road where you turn left, joining the Coast Path. The woodland on the left is Llanrhidian Hill Nature Reserve, owned and managed by the Wildlife Trust for South and West Wales.

The road ends and becomes a path that crosses the top of a field and at a junction of paths, take the route indicated by the blue marker that runs along the top of the field with the salt marsh on your right. This comes to a gate after which there is a view of Weobley Castle ahead. Ignore the permissive footpath that climbs up through Leason Wood and carry straight on in the direction of the castle.

The path starts to climb up the hill on a very old stony lane, then take a footpath on the right towards **Landimore**. This enters a large field which you leave halfway along via a stile in the fence with a blue Coast Path arrow. Continue along to a track which you cross over and then take the footpath on the left which leads up left edge of the grassy field in the valley to join the track.

Turn left here if you wish to explore **Weobley Castle** (see Walk 29). The Castle is well worth exploring and offers a superb view of the Loughor Estuary.

ARTHUR'S STONE AND GREAT CARN

Arthur's Stone/Maen Ceti with the Burry Estuary and Carmarthenshire in the distance

Arthur's Stone is a Neolithic burial chamber, or cromlech, dramatically situated on Cefn Bryn. It dates from 2500BC and consists of a huge quartz conglomerate boulder supported on nine uprights. Legend has it that while walking in Llanelli, King Arthur found a stone in his shoe and hurled it all the way from Carmarthenshire, straight over the Burry Estuary, to Cefn Bryn. Touched by the hand of King Arthur, the stone physically grew with pride and the surrounding stones raised it high with admiration.

The capstone has been estimated to weigh more than 25.4 tonnes. For many years it was casually assumed to be Devonian conglomerate, the same rock type that comprises much of the hill itself. Detailed study, however, has shown that it is actually millstone grit, the nearest outcrop of which is some 30 miles away on the northern edge of the coalfield. This block is therefore not in situ, but an erratic, carried here by the glaciers of the last Ice Age. The two-chambered burial tomb would have been constructed by excavating under the rock and inserting the upright supporting stones as they dug.

The large circular flat-topped mound of big stones 100m to the west is known as the Great Carn and is the largest of the numerous Bronze Age cairns found on Cefn Bryn.

View through the window in Weobley Castle

Otherwise, turn right and follow the road to a junction where you turn left and then right to **Windmill Farm**. Just past the house there is a gate with a footpath sign. Go into the field and keep close to the hedge on your right and to another gate where there is an impressive 3.2m-high quartz conglomerate standing stone called **Samson's Jack**. This dates from the Bronze Age around 2000–1000BC.

Continue following the fence on your right and follow the signs to the main North Gower road where you turn right. Follow this to the bottom of the valley in **Stembridge** and turn left, marked Fairy Hill Restaurant, and then left onto a footpath that crosses the field diagonally up to the left.

Follow the hedge to another stile and to the tarmac road at Hillend where you turn left and then right through a gate. Turn left where you soon join a track and take the one that climbs the hillside, ignoring the one on the left. Stay on this bridleway heading for the trig point on **Cefn Bryn**. There are around 60 piles of stones on Cefn Bryn. Some of these are Bronze Age while others were made by farmers clearing the fields.

Continue along the ridge back to the start.

WALK 29

Llanrhidian and Weobley Castle

Start/finish	St Illtyd's Church, Llanrhidian (SS 4976 9223)
Distance	5km (3.2 miles)
Total ascent	60m
Time	1hr 30min
Refreshments	Pubs in Llanrhidian

An easy walk cuts across farmland from St Illtyd's Church at Llanrhidian to Weobley Castle, giving excellent views across the salt marsh. The return is along the Coast Path where there is plenty of bird life to see over the marsh and fine woodland borders the landward side of the route. You have a choice of two pubs to reward your venture into this beautiful and tranquil area of Gower. St Illtyd's Church, with its leper stone in the porch, is well worth a visit at the start of the walk.

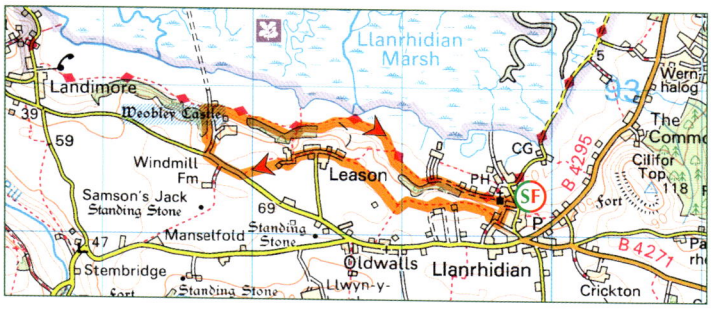

On the road with **St Illtyd's Church** on your right, walk up the hill in **Llanrhidian** and turn immediately right up the narrow lane between the houses. Turn right at the T-junction and carry straight on following the footpath sign.

Shortly after you reach a small crest. Look to the right to see the hill fort on Cilifor, with its earth bank ramparts (see Walk 30). The path continues to a farm where you go straight across the concrete yard and back onto the footpath to a stile. Continue in the same direction on the permissive footpath, ignoring the yellow sign on the left, and this soon rejoins the right of way after Penrhallt Farm.

ST ILLTYD'S CHURCH, LLANRHIDIAN

The leper stone, Llanrhidian Church

Although dedicated to St Illtyd, the church is reputed to have been founded by the Celtic saint St Rhidian during the sixth century. The current building, on the site of the early Celtic foundation, dates from around 1300, but was extensively renovated in 1858 with the nave being completely rebuilt.

A significant historical find, dating from the ninth century, was unearthed from the ground beside the tower in 1880. Known as the 'leper stone', this 2m-long rectangular block of limestone was moved to the porch for safe-keeping in 1910. Carvings upon one side depict two stylised human figures surrounded by a pair of grotesque-looking animals.

The church has strong links with the order of the Knights of St John Jerusalem, the Hospitallers. The large tower was intended to provide refuge for the villagers during the Anglo-Norman conquest of Wales. On one side of the tower parapet is a raised platform called the Parson's Bed; this was the hearth for a beacon fire to warn the locals of enemies approaching by land or sea.

Cross the next stile and keep the hedge on your left to another stile where you turn right along the hedge in the field, ignoring the footpath that goes straight on. Cut across the fields to the farm at **Leason** Wood. Do not cross over the first stile in the fence but carry on to the next stile and cross into the farm lane, turn left and carry on along the road ignoring the turning on the left.

When this track comes to some houses, turn left at the brown Gower Walks sign, ignoring the yellow footpath sign straight ahead. Follow the track around to the right of the bungalow and follow the brown signs over the fields to the road. Turn right and then right again where you see the sign for Weobley Castle, and then left a few metres afterwards and along the fence on the right side of the valley.

WEOBLEY CASTLE

Weobley Castle

Weobley Castle is Gower's most spectacular building, set atop a cliff overlooking the Loughor Estuary. It was a fortified manor house, designed for comfort rather than defence. The early history of the small lordship of Weobley is uncertain but it is likely that it was one of the first Norman holdings in Gower, though the earliest reference is in a charter of liberties issued in 1306.

Weobley was one of the 12 'ancient knight's fees', whose lords held a privileged position within the wider English community of the Marcher lordship of Gower. Most of the fees were in the south of Gower, the area of primary Norman occupation, and it is likely that Weobley originally lay further south. Additional lands, including the site of the present castle, were probably acquired in the 13th century.

David de la Bere, a steward to the De Braose Lord of Gower in 1292 and 1304, acquired 'Leason' in 1304, and his son Adam witnessed a deed signed at Weobley Castle in 1318. David is recorded as having been attacked by the men of Henry, Earl of Lancaster, and is the most likely builder of the castle.

Turn right on to the Coast Path at the bottom of the field and follow it back to Llanrhidian where it changes into a tarmac road. The woodland on the right is Llanrhidian Hill Nature Reserve, owned and managed by the Wildlife Trust for South and West Wales.

With the church tower in front of you, take the footpath off to the right behind the ponds in the gardens to the church and back to the start in **Llanrhidian**.

WALK 30

Llanrhidian, Cilifor Top, Parc le Breos and Cefn Bryn

Start/finish	St Illtyd's Church, Llanrhidian (SS 4976 9223)
Distance	14km (8.7 miles)
Total ascent	310m
Time	4hr
Refreshments	Pubs and garage in Llanrhidian

This is a good day's walk that ascends Cilifor Top, a fine vantage point for superb views of the Loughor Estuary and north Gower and the site of a large hill fort. A cross-country traverse of the peninsula via Park Woods and Parc le Breos brings you to Cefn Bryn and the magnificent panorama of the south Gower coast. The return leg passes Broad Pool, an interesting nature reserve for birds and insects. St Illtyd's Church, with the leper stone in the porch, is well worth a visit at the start of this walk (see Walk 29).

On the road with the church on your left in **Llanrhidian**, drop down the hill and bear right just after the Dolphin Inn. Take the next footpath on the right just before a house. Once in the field, turn right and follow the fence to the stile that brings you to the road.

Cross over and go slightly to the right and follow the fence on the right to a stile. Cross over, turn left and follow the fence to another stile. Strike up left to a flatter area over the first hill fort rampart. Turn right and then left to bring you to the summit of **Cilifor Top**. There are excellent views to the west of Llanrhidian village, the salt marsh and Whiteford Burrows, and further left to Llanmadoc Hill and Rhossili Down.

CIL IFOR PROMONTORY FORT

Cil Ifor is the finest multivallate hill fort on Gower, comprising three large ramparts and ditches enclosing the steep-sided hill, a so-called terrace camp, and is unique in Gower. Dating from no later than the first century BC, this large Iron Age defensive settlement enclosing three hectares would have had substantial influence on the surrounding area.

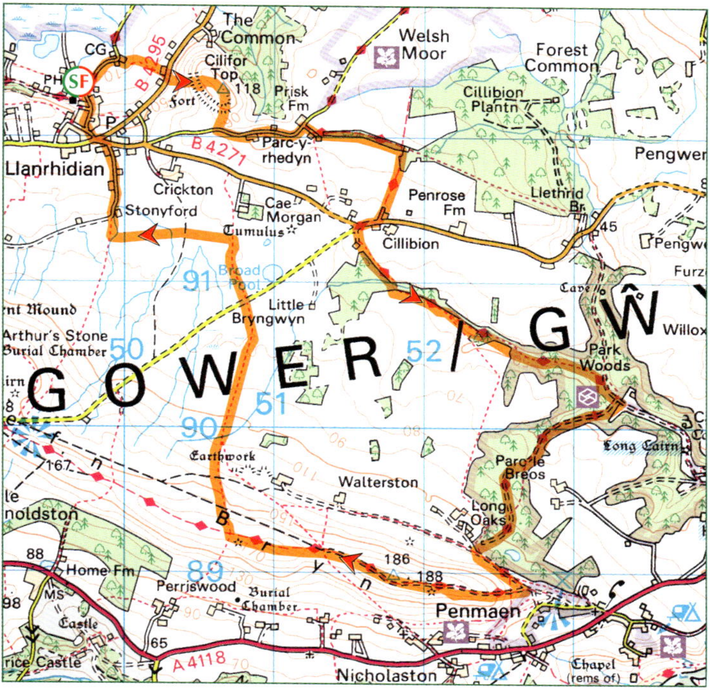

WALK 30 – LLANRHIDIAN, CILIFOR TOP, PARC LE BREOS AND CEFN BRYN

View of north Gower from the ascent of Cilifor Top

Follow the ridge to the trig point and continue to one of the earth ramparts; follow this down until you reach a stile in the fence ahead. Turn left along the road to **Prisk Farm** and turn right, signposted Cillibion, to a crossroads where you turn right. At the end of the bridleway, turn right at the road opposite North Road Service Station in **Cillibion**, cross over and turn left, signposted Cefn Bryn, and immediately left again down the track to the house and onto the Gower Way at marker stone 17.

Cross over the stile to the left of the house and follow the edge of Decoy Wood over a number of stiles, with the impassable sunken track on your right. At the farm track turn right and cross the stream. Turn left once in the field and follow the fence on your left, still on the Gower Way, into the valley of Lodge Cwm. Look out for the limekiln on your left and a cliff of Carboniferous limestone behind.

You may notice that the stream we were following earlier has disappeared with no evidence of surface water in the valley. It is now running underground in passageways in the limestone.

The track merges with one joining from the left and shortly after you come to a crossroads. It is worth making a short detour by continuing straight on down the valley for 500m to see Cathole Cave and Parc Cwm Long Cairn (see Walk 7).

From the crossroads, turn right and follow the forestry track through **Parc le Breos** (see Walk 7). Pass through the swing gate, turn left and then right on the

Water lilies in flower at Broad Pool

WALK 30 – LLANRHIDIAN, CILIFOR TOP, PARC LE BREOS AND CEFN BRYN

Gower Way to **Cefn Bryn** (see Walk 8). Follow the track westwards to a pile of stones forming a cairn. Look back to see Three Cliffs Bay and the headlands culminating in the stepped profile of Pwlldu Head. To the right is Oxwich Bay and Oxwich Point.

Continue along the ridge to the summit. Turn right where the path flattens out along an indistinct path in the direction of Cilifor Top. Cut across the moorland, over a track coming across the hillside and, where there is a boulder of millstone grit, follow a small furrow in the hillside first left and then right, heading for the corner of the field and woodland, again in line with Cilifor Top.

Where the field meets the common at a stream, take the wide grassy track in the direction of Broad Pool. When you reach the road, cross over and pick up the footpath sign to the left of the nature reserve of **Broad Pool** (see Walk 8). Strike across the moor to Moormills, an interesting area where a number of streams have exposed the underlying rock and drain through swallet holes, disappearing underground. Continue over the moor, heading for a dogleg in the pylons and to a stile in the fence just around the corner.

Over the stile, bear right and follow the lane with the farmhouse of **Stonyford** on your right. This brings you to the main road at the garage in **Llanrhidian** where you turn left and then right down the hill and back to the start.

APPENDIX A
Local points of interest index

Arthur's Stone and Great Carn (Walk 28)
Bacon Hole (Walk 4)
Berry Wood (Walk 10)
Bishopston Valley (Walk 3)
Broad Pool (Walk 8)
Burry Holms (Walk 23)
Cairn Circle, Rhossili Down (Walk 22)
Cathole Cave (Walk 7)
Cefn Bryn and Talbot's Road (Walk 8)
Cil Ifor promontory fort (Walk 30)
Culver Hole, Port Eynon (Walk 17)
Deborah's Hole Nature Reserve (Walk 17)
Dollar Ship, The (Walk 20)
Dylan Thomas, Rhossili (Walk 21)
Goat's Hole, Paviland (Walk 16)
Great Carn (Walk 8)
Hardings Down hill fort (Walk 22)
Helvetia, The (Walk 18)
Millwood (Walk 11)
Minchin Hole (Walk 4)
Mumbles Train (Walk 1)
Oxwich Castle (Walk 13)
Oxwich Limestone Quarrying (Walk 13)
Oxwich National Nature Reserve (Walk 12)
Oystermouth Castle (Walk 1)
Parc Cwm long cairn (Walk 7)
Parc le Breos (Walk 7)
Park Woods (Walk 8)
Penmaen Castle (Walk 9)
Pennard Castle (Walk 5)
Penrice Estate (Walk 11)
Pwlldu Bay Smuggling (Walk 3)
Pwlldu Quarrying (Walk 2)
Rhossili Rectory (Walk 18)
Rhossili Quarries (Walk 19)
Salt House, Port Eynon (Walk 15)
Solifluction terrace (Walk 22)
South Gower Coast Nature Reserves (Walk 17)
St Andrew's Church, Penrice (Walk 14)
St Cattwg's Church, Port Eynon (Walk 15)
St Illtyd's Church, Illston (Walk 6)
St Illtyd's Church, Llanrhidian (Walk 29)
St Illtyd's Church, Oxwich (Walk 14)
Sweyne's Howes, Rhossili Down (Walk 21)
Tankeylake Moor (Walk 20)
The Bulwark (Walk 24)
Viel, The (Walk 21)
Weobley Castle (Walk 29)
Whiteford National Nature Reserve (Walk 25)
Whiteford Lighthouse (Walk 25)
Worms Head (Walk 19)
Worms Head Causeway (Walk 19)

APPENDIX B
Useful websites

Heritage and history
National Trust
https://www.nationaltrust.org.uk/visit/wales/gower

The Glamorgan–Gwent Archaeological Trust
www.ggat.org.uk

Environment and wildlife
Cyfoeth Naturiol Cymru Natural Resources Wales
https://naturalresources.wales/

Wildlife Trust for South and West Wales
www.welshwildlife.org

Glamorgan Birds
www.glamorganbirds.org.uk

Carmarthenshire Bird Club
https://carmarthenshirebird.club/

Tourist and general information
Cyngor Abertawe Swansea Council
www.swansea.gov.uk/gowernationallandscape

Swansea Bay
www.visitswanseabay.com

Visit Wales
https://www.visitmidwales.co.uk/showmewales/south-west-wales

Public transport
Traveline Cymru
https://www.traveline.cymru/
tel 0800 464 00 00

DOWNLOAD THE GPX FILES

All the routes in this guide are available for download from:

www.cicerone.co.uk/1284/GPX

as standard format GPX files. You should be able to load them into most online GPX systems and mobile devices, whether GPS or smartphone. You may need to convert the file into your preferred format using a conversion programme such as gpsvisualizer.com or one of the many other such websites and programmes.

When you follow this link, you will be asked for your email address and where you purchased the guidebook, and have the option to subscribe to the Cicerone e-newsletter.

www.cicerone.co.uk

LISTING OF CICERONE GUIDES

BRITISH ISLES CHALLENGES, COLLECTIONS AND ACTIVITIES

Great Walks on the England Coast Path
Map and Compass
The Big Rounds
The Book of the Bivvy
The Book of the Bothy
The Mountains of England and Wales
 Vol 1 — Wales
 Vol 2 — England
The National Trails
Walking the End to End Trail
Cycling Land's End to John o' Groats

LAKE DISTRICT

Bikepacking in the Lake District
Cycling in the Lake District
Joss Naylor's Lakes, Meres and Waters of the Lake District
Lake District Winter Climbs
Lake District: High Level and Fell Walks
Lake District: Low Level and Lake Walks
Mountain Biking in the Lake District
Outdoor Adventures with Children — Lake District
Scrambles in the Lake District — North
Scrambles in the Lake District — South
Trail and Fell Running in the Lake District
Walking The Cumbria Way
Walking the Lake District Fells
 — Borrowdale
 — Buttermere
 — Coniston
 — Keswick
 — Langdale
 — Mardale and the Far East
 — Patterdale
 — Wasdale
Walking the Tour of the Lake District

NORTH-WEST ENGLAND AND THE ISLE OF MAN

Walking the King Charles III England Coast Path: North West
Walking the King Charles III England Coast Path: North West
 — Cumbria Map Booklet
 — Lancashire and Merseyside Map Booklet
Cycling the Pennine Bridleway
Walking the Pennine Way
Walking the Pennine Way Map Booklet
Isle of Man Coastal Path
The Lune Valley and Howgills
Walking in Cumbria's Eden Valley
Walking in Lancashire
Walking in the Forest of Bowland and Pendle
Walking on the Isle of Man
Walking on the West Pennine Moors
Walking the Ribble Way
Hadrian's Wall Path
Hadrian's Wall Path Map Booklet

The Coast to Coast Cycle Route
The Coast to Coast Map Booklet
The Coast to Coast Walk

NORTH-EAST ENGLAND, YORKSHIRE DALES AND PENNINES

Walking the Dales Way
The Dales Way Map Booklet
Cycling the Reivers Route
Cycling the Way of the Roses
Cycling in the Yorkshire Dales
Great Mountain Days in the Pennines
Mountain Biking in the Yorkshire Dales
The Cleveland Way and the Yorkshire Wolds Way
The Cleveland Way Map Booklet
The North York Moors
Trail and Fell Running in the Yorkshire Dales
Walking in County Durham
Walking in Northumberland
Walking in Northumberland
Walking in the North Pennines
Walking in the Yorkshire Dales
 — North and East
 — South and West
Walking St Cuthbert's Way
Walking St Oswald's Way and Northumberland Coast Path

DERBYSHIRE, PEAK DISTRICT AND MIDLANDS

Cycling in the Peak District
Dark Peak Walks
Scrambles in the Dark Peak
Walking in Derbyshire
Walking in the Peak District
 — White Peak East
 — White Peak West

SOUTHERN ENGLAND

20 Classic Sportive Rides in South East England
20 Classic Sportive Rides in South West England
Bikepacking — South East Gravel
Cycling in the Cotswolds
Mountain Biking on the North Downs
South West Coast Path Map Booklet
 — Vol 1: Minehead to St Ives
 — Vol 2: St Ives to Plymouth
 — Vol 3: Plymouth to Poole
Suffolk Coast and Heath Walks
The Cotswold Way
The Cotswold Way Map Booklet
The Kennet and Avon Canal
The Lea Valley Walk
The Lea Valley Walk
The North Downs Way
North Downs Way Map Booklet
The Peddars Way and Norfolk Coast Path
The Pilgrims' Way
The Ridgeway National Trail

The Ridgeway Map Booklet
The South Downs Way
The South Downs Way Map Booklet
The Thames Path
The Thames Path Map Booklet
The Two Moors Way
Two Moors Way Map Booklet
Walking Hampshire's Test Way
Walking in Essex
Walking in Kent
Walking in London
Walking in Norfolk
Walking in the Chilterns
Walking in the Cotswolds
Walking in the Isles of Scilly
Walking in the New Forest
Walking in the North Wessex Downs
Walking on Dartmoor
Walking on Guernsey
Walking on Jersey
Walking on the Isle of Wight
Walking the Dartmoor Way
Walking the Jurassic Coast
Walking the Sarsen Way
Walking the South West Coast Path
Walks in the South Downs National Park

WALES AND WELSH BORDERS

Cycle Touring in Wales
Cycling Lon Las Cymru
Great Mountain Days in Snowdonia
Hillwalking in Shropshire
Mountain Walking in Snowdonia
Offa's Dyke Path
Offa's Dyke Map Booklet
Scrambles in Snowdonia
Snowdonia: 30 Low-level and Easy Walks
 — North
 — South
The Cambrian Way
The Pembrokeshire Coast Path
Pembrokeshire Coast Path Map Booklet
The Snowdonia Way
The Wye Valley Walk
Walking Glyndwr's Way
Walking in Carmarthenshire
Walking in Gower
Walking in Pembrokeshire
Walking in the Brecon Beacons
Walking on Gower
Walking the Severn Way
Walking the Shropshire Way
Walking the Wales Coast Path

SHORT WALKS SERIES

15 Short Walks in Dumfries and Galloway
15 Short Walks in Perthshire North — Pitlochry, Aberfeldy and Dunkeld
15 Short Walks in the Scottish Borders
15 Short Walks in the Trossachs — Callander and Aberfoyle
15 Short Walks on the Isle of Mull
15 Short Walks on the Isle of Skye

15 Short Walks on the Orkney Islands
15 Short Walks on the Shetland Islands
15 Short Walks Hadrian's Wall
15 Short Walks in the Lake District
  — Keswick, Borrowdale and Buttermere
  — Windermere Ambleside and Grasmere
  — Coniston and Langdale
15 Short Walks in Arnside and Silverdale
15 Short Walks in the Ribble Valley
15 Short Walks in Nidderdale
15 Short Walks in Northumberland — Wooler, Rothbury, Alnwick and the coast
15 Short Walks in the Yorkshire Dales
  — Grassington, Skipton, Malham and Ilkley
  — Sedbergh, Kirkby Lonsdale and Ingleton
15 Short Walks in the Peak District — Bakewell and the White Peak
15 Short Walks in the Peak District — Edale and the Hope Valley
15 Short Walks on the Malvern Hills
15 Short Walks Cheddar and the Mendips
15 Short Walks in Cornwall
  — Newquay and the North Coast
  — Falmouth and the Lizard
  — Land's End and Penzance
15 Short Walks in Norfolk — Broads and Coast
15 Short Walks in South Devon — Salcombe, Brixham and the coast
15 Short Walks in the South Downs — Brighton, Eastbourne and Arundel
15 Short Walks in the Surrey Hills
15 Short Walks on Dartmoor North — Okehampton and Chagford
15 Short Walks on Dartmoor South — Ivybridge and Princetown
15 Short Walks on Exmoor
15 Short Walks on the Isle of Wight
15 Short Walks Winchester
15 Short Walks in Bannau Brycheiniog — Brecon Beacons
15 Short Walks in Pembrokeshire — Tenby and the south
15 Short Walks in the Forest of Dean

SCOTLAND

Ben Nevis and Glen Coe
Cycling in the Hebrides
Cycling in the Hebrides
Cycling the North Coast 500
Great Mountain Days in Scotland
Mountain Biking in Southern and Central Scotland
Mountain Biking in West and North West Scotland
Not the West Highland Way: A Mountain High Way
Scotland
Scotland's Best Small Mountains
Scottish Wild Country Backpacking
Skye Munros
Skye's Cuillin Ridge Traverse
The Borders Abbeys Way
The Hebridean Way
The Hebrides
The Isle of Skye
The Skye Trail
The Southern Upland Way
The West Highland Way
West Highland Way Map Booklet
Walking Ben Lawers, Rannoch and Atholl
Walking in the Cairngorms
Walking in the Pentland Hills
Walking in the Scottish Borders
Walking in the Southern Uplands
Walking in Torridon, Fisherfield, Fannichs and An Teallach
Walking Loch Lomond and the Trossachs
Walking on Arran
Walking on Harris and Lewis
Walking on Jura, Islay and Colonsay
Walking on Mull, Coll and Tiree
Walking on Rum and the Small Isles
Walking on the Orkney and Shetland Isles
Walking on Uist and Barra
Walking Rum and the Small Isles
Walking the Cape Wrath Trail
Walking the Corbetts
  Vol 1 — South of the Great Glen
  Vol 2 — North of the Great Glen
Walking the Fife Pilgrim Way
Walking the Galloway Hills
Walking the Great Glen Way
Walking the Great Glen Way Map Booklet
Walking the John o' Groats Trail
Walking the Munros
  Vol 1 — Southern, Central and Western Highlands
  Vol 2 — Northern Highlands and the Cairngorms
Winter Climbs in the Cairngorms
Winter Climbs: Ben Nevis and Glen Coe

ALPS CROSS-BORDER ROUTES

100 Hut Walks in the Alps
Alpine Ski Mountaineering Vol 1 — Western Alps
Hiking the Tour of Monte Rosa
The Karnischer Hohenweg
The Tour of the Bernina
Trail Running — Chamonix and the Mont Blanc region
Trekking Chamonix to Zermatt
Trekking in the Alps
Trekking in the Silvretta and Ratikon Alps
Trekking Munich to Venice
Trekking the Tour du Mont Blanc
Tour du Mont Blanc Map Booklet
Walking in the Alps

FRANCE, BELGIUM AND LUXEMBOURG

Camino de Santiago — Via Podiensis
Chamonix Mountain Adventures
Cycling London to Paris
Cycling the Canal de la Garonne
Cycling the Canal du Midi
Mont Blanc Walks
Mountain Adventures in the Maurienne
Short Treks on Corsica
The GR5 Trail — Through the French Alps
The GR5 Trail — Vosges and Jura
The Moselle Cycle Route
Trekking in the Vanoise
Trekking the Cathar Way
Trekking the GR10
Trekking the GR20 Corsica
Trekking the Robert Louis Stevenson Trail
Via Ferratas of the French Alps
Walking in Provence — East
Walking in Provence — West
Walking in the Auvergne
Walking in the Briançonnais
Walking in the Dordogne
Walking in the Haute Savoie: North
Walking in the Haute Savoie: South
Walking on Corsica
Walking the Brittany Coast Path
The GR5 Trail — Benelux and Lorraine
Walking in the Ardennes
The River Loire Cycle Route
The River Rhone Cycle Route
Cycling the Route des Grandes Alpes

PYRENEES AND FRANCE/SPAIN CROSS-BORDER ROUTES

Shorter Treks in the Pyrenees
The Pyrenean Haute Route
The Pyrenees
Trekking the Cami dels Bons Homes
Trekking the GR11 Trail
Walks and Climbs in the Pyrenees

SPAIN AND PORTUGAL

Camino de Santiago: Camino Frances
Coastal Walks in Andalucia
Costa Blanca Mountain Adventures
Cycling the Camino de Santiago
Mountain Walking in Mallorca
Mountain Walking in Southern Catalunya
Spain's Sendero Historico: The GR1
The Andalucian Coast to Coast Walk
The Camino del Norte and Camino Primitivo
The Camino Ingles and Ruta do Mar
The Mountains Around Nerja
The Mountains of Ronda and Grazalema
The Sierras of Extremadura
Trekking in Mallorca
Trekking in the Canary Islands
Trekking the GR7 in Andalucia
Walking and Trekking in the Sierra Nevada
Walking in Andalucia
Walking in Catalunya — Barcelona
Walking in Catalunya — Girona Pyrenees
Walking in the Picos de Europa
Walking La Via de la Plata and Camino Sanabres
Walking on Gran Canaria
Walking on La Gomera and El Hierro
Walking on La Palma
Walking on Lanzarote and Fuerteventura

Walking on Tenerife
Walking on the Costa Blanca
Walking the Camino dos Faros
Portugal's Rota Vicentina
The Camino Portugues
Walking in Portugal
Walking in the Algarve
Walking in the Algarve
Walking on Madeira
Walking on the Azores
Cycling the Ruta Via de la Plata

SWITZERLAND
Switzerland's Jura Crest Trail
The Swiss Alps
Tour of the Jungfrau Region
Trekking the Swiss Via Alpina
Walking in Arolla and Zinal
Walking in the Bernese Oberland — Jungfrau region
Walking in the Engadine — Switzerland
Walking in Ticino
Walking in Zermatt and Saas-Fee

GERMANY
Hiking and Cycling in the Black Forest
The Danube Cycleway Vol 1
The Rhine Cycle Route
The Westweg
Walking in the Bavarian Alps
The Elbe Cycle Route

POLAND, SLOVAKIA, ROMANIA, HUNGARY AND BULGARIA
The Danube Cycleway Vol 2
The High Tatras
The Mountains of Romania

SCANDINAVIA, ICELAND AND GREENLAND
Hiking in Norway
— North
— South
Trekking the Kungsleden
Trekking in Greenland — The Arctic Circle Trail
Walking and Trekking in Iceland

SLOVENIA, CROATIA, SERBIA, MONTENEGRO AND ALBANIA
Hiking Slovenia's Juliana Trail
Mountain Biking in Slovenia
The Islands of Croatia
The Julian Alps of Slovenia
The Mountains of Montenegro
The Peaks of the Balkans Trail
The Slovene Mountain Trail
Walking in Slovenia: The Karavanke
Walking the Julian Alps of Slovenia
Walks and Treks in Croatia

ITALY
Alta Via 1 — Trekking in the Dolomites
Alta Via 2 — Trekking in the Dolomites
Day Walks in the Dolomites
Italy's Grande Traversata delle Alpi
Ski Touring and Snowshoeing in the Dolomites
The Way of St Francis: Via di Francesco
Trekking Gran Paradiso: Alta Via 2
Trekking in the Apennines
Trekking the Giants' Trail: Alta Via 1 through the Italian Pennine Alps
Via Ferratas of the Italian Dolomites
— Vol 1
— Vol 2
Walking Gran Paradiso National Park
Walking in Abruzzo
Walking in Italy's Cinque Terre
Walking in Italy's Stelvio National Park
Walking in Sicily
Walking in the Aosta Valley
Walking in the Dolomites
Walking in Tuscany
Walking in Umbria
Walking Lake Como and Maggiore
Walking Lake Garda and Iseo
Walking on the Amalfi Coast
Walking the Cammino Materano
Walking the Via Francigena Pilgrim Route
— Part 1
— Part 2
— Part 3
— Part 4
Walks and Treks in the Maritime Alps

IRELAND
The Wild Atlantic Way and Western Ireland
Walking the Kerry Way
Walking the Wicklow Way

INTERNATIONAL CHALLENGES, COLLECTIONS AND ACTIVITIES
Europe's High Points
Pocket First Aid and Wilderness Medicine

AUSTRIA
Innsbruck Mountain Adventures
Trekking Austria's Adlerweg
Trekking in Austria's Hohe Tauern
Trekking in Austria's Stubai Alps
Trekking in Austria's Zillertal Alps
Walking in Austria
Walking in the Salzkammergut: the Austrian Lake District

MEDITERRANEAN
Trekking in Greece
Walking and Trekking in Zagori
Walking and Trekking on Corfu
Walking on the Greek Islands — the Cyclades
Walking in Cyprus
Walking on Malta

HIMALAYA
8000 metres
Annapurna
Everest: A Trekker's Guide
Trekking in the Indian Himalayas
Trekking in the Karakoram

NORTH AMERICA
Hiking and Cycling the California Missions Trail
Hiking the Pacific Crest Trail
The John Muir Trail

SOUTH AMERICA
Aconcagua and the Southern Andes
Hiking and Biking Peru's Inca Trails
Trekking in Torres del Paine

AFRICA
Climbing Toubkal
Kilimanjaro
Walking in the Drakensberg
Walks and Scrambles in the Moroccan Anti-Atlas

NEW ZEALAND AND AUSTRALIA
Hiking the Overland Track

CHINA, JAPAN AND ASIA
Hiking and Trekking in the Japan Alps and Mount Fuji
Hiking in Hong Kong
Japan's Kumano Kodo Pilgrimage
Trekking in Bhutan
Trekking in Ladakh
Trekking in Tajikistan
Trekking in the Himalaya

TECHNIQUES
Fastpacking
The Mountain Hut Book

MINI GUIDES
Alpine Flowers
Navigation

MOUNTAIN LITERATURE
A Walk in the Clouds
Abode of the Gods
Fifty Years of Adventure
The Pennine Way — the Path, the People, the Journey
Unjustifiable Risk?

For full information on all our guides, books and eBooks,
visit our website:
www.cicerone.co.uk

CICERONE

Trust Cicerone to guide your next adventure, wherever it may be around the world...

Discover guides for hiking, mountain walking, backpacking, trekking, trail running, cycling and mountain biking, ski touring, climbing and scrambling in Britain, Europe and worldwide.

Connect with Cicerone online and find inspiration.

- buy books and ebooks
- articles, advice and trip reports
- GPX files and updates
- regular newsletter

cicerone.co.uk